Amtrak

Amtrak
The National Railroad Passenger Corporation

George W. Hilton

American Enterprise Institute for Public Policy Research
Washington, D.C.

George W. Hilton is professor of economics at the University of California, Los Angeles, and an adjunct scholar of the American Enterprise Institute.

Library of Congress Cataloging in Publication Data

Hilton, George Woodman.
AMTRAK : the National Railroad Passenger Corporation.

(AEI evaluative studies in economic policy) (AEI studies ; 266)
    1. Amtrak.   2. Railroads—United States—Passenger traffic.
I. Series: American Enterprise Institute for Public Policy Research.
AEI evaluative studies in economic policy. II. Series:
American Enterprise Institute for Public Policy Research.
AEI studies ; 266.
HE2583.H54   385'.22'0973   79-25118
ISBN 0-8447-3369-5

AEI Studies 266

Printed in the United States of America

171848

CONTENTS

1
The Life Cycle of
Rail Passenger Service

The National Railroad Passenger Corporation, established by Congress in 1970, began operating a federal network of intercity passenger trains the following year. Amtrak, as the corporation came to be called, was Congress's response to forces that threatened the imminent extinction of intercity rail passenger service in America. As such, it was a new departure in public policy: never before had Congress directly intervened in the economy to save a service that was being replaced by alternatives.

The life cycle of rail passenger service had approximated the standard pattern of output of industries over their life cycles.[1] Most early railroads were built with the expectation of moving passengers and agricultural products to and from steamboats on the East Coast, the Great Lakes, or the inland river system. In the first half of the nineteenth century, it had generally been believed that the advantages of steamboats in both cost and quality of service would make them the country's dominant mode of passenger and freight transport indefinitely. However, with the completion of the main lines of the Pennsylvania and New York Central railroad systems between East Coast ports and Chicago in the 1850s, this belief began to be questioned. The introduction of sleeping cars, dining cars, steel underframe equipment, and train vestibules in the second half of the century gave the passenger train a definite superiority over the steamboat for long-distance travel. By 1900 the railroad train had attracted the great majority of long-distance passengers, drawing them from inland river packets in particular.

---

[1] On the ubiquity of a pattern of increase in output at an increasing rate, increase at a decreasing rate, decrease at an increasing rate, and decrease at a decreasing rate, see Walther Hoffman, *British Industry, 1700–1950* (Oxford: Basil Blackwell, 1955).

The passenger train probably reached its peak share around the mid-1890s when it is thought to have provided some 95 percent of intercity trips. In 1887–1888 Frank J. Sprague perfected the electric street car, thus providing the first technology that could compete for significant numbers of railroad passengers. In the form of rural trolley lines in New England, electric railways began diverting short-distance passengers from the railroads soon afterward. And, mostly after 1899, the interurbans—more substantial, higher speed electric railways—began proliferating in the Midwest and elsewhere.[2] However, these carriers, which did not prove successful in the long run, merely slowed the rate of increase in railroad passenger volume. Both passengers and passenger-miles on the railroads peaked just after World War I. In 1920, as table 1 indicates, the railroads carried approximately 1.27 billion passengers for a total of 47.4 billion passenger-miles.

That year saw the highest volume in railroad history. The proliferation of automobiles and the development of a federal system of hard-surfaced highways in the 1920s brought the automobile within a single decade to domination of intercity passenger transport, a pattern that has persisted ever since. By 1929 the railroads had lost 38.1 percent of their passengers and 34.3 percent of their passenger-miles. Short-distance passengers converted to the automobile more rapidly than long-distance. The motor bus, too, which made its first significant inroads into railroad passenger volume in this period, originally carried mostly short-distance passengers. Consequently, the average distance of railroad trips rose continuously as the decline progressed. In 1929 the passenger train still dominated the long-distance common carrier market so overwhelmingly that it was almost universally expected to survive indefinitely. Most long-distance trains remained profitable—enough so that although many local trains experienced losses, rail passenger operations as a whole were profitable through 1929.

The Great Depression introduced a cyclical element that aggravated the secular forces operating against the passenger train. At the beginning of the Depression in 1930, passenger service began to produce a net deficit for the railroads. By 1933 the number of passengers had fallen to 435 million and passenger-miles to 16.4 billion, only a third of the 1920 levels. An improvement in business conditions in the second half of the 1930s combined with the introduction of lightweight, streamlined, and air-conditioned equipment, improvements in schedule speeds, and the introduction of the diesel locomotive

---

[2] See George W. Hilton and John F. Due, *The Electric Interurban Railways in America* (Stanford, Calif.: Stanford University Press, 1960).

TABLE 1
Output and Financial Performance of American Railroad Passenger Service, 1920–1970

Year	Passengers (thousands)	Passenger-Miles (thousands)	Net Revenue[a] (thousands of dollars)	Passenger Deficit as Percentage of Freight Net Revenue
1920	1,269,913	47,369,906		
1921	1,061,131	37,705,737		
1922	989,509	35,811,046		
1923	1,008,538	38,294,178		
1924	950,459	36,368,290		
1925	901,963	36,166,973		
1926	874,589	35,672,729		
1927	840,030	33,797,754		
1928	798,476	31,717,566		
1929	786,432	31,164,739		
1930	707,987	26,875,642		
1931	599,227	21,933,345		
1932	480,718	16,997,426		
1933	434,848	16,368,635		
1934	452,176	18,068,635		
1935	448,059	18,509,497		
1936	492,493	22,459,781	−233,327	26.2
1937	499,688	24,695,214	−241,591	29.2
1938	454,508	21,656,918	−255,263	40.8
1939	454,032	22,712,941	−250,934	29.9
1940	456,088	23,815,598	−262,058	27.8
1941	488,668	29,406,250	−226,029	18.5
1942	672,420	53,747,029	89,329	—
1943	887,694	87,924,994	279,790	—
1944	915,817	95,662,501	234,103	—
1945	897,384	91,826,353	230,060	—
1946	794,824	64,753,699	−139,736	18.4
1947	706,551	45,972,245	−426,526	35.4
1948	645,535	41,224,319	−559,782	35.9
1949	556,741	35,133,300	−649,627	48.6
1950	488,019	31,790,470	−508,508	32.9
1951	485,468	34,640,031	−680,822	41.9
1952	470,979	34,033,245	−642,390	37.3
1953	458,252	31,678,951	−705,538	38.9
1954	440,770	29,309,861	−669,533	43.4

(Table continues on next page)

TABLE 1 (continued)

Year	Passengers (thousands)	Passenger-Miles (thousands)	Net Revenue[a] (thousands of dollars)	Passenger Deficit as Percentage of Freight Net Revenue
1955	433,308	28,547,877	−636,693	36.1
1956	429,994	28,215,728	−696,938	39.5
1957	412,625	25,914,446	−723,483	44.0
1958	381,623	23,295,262	−591,543	35.7
1959	353,647	22,074,718	−523,692	32.8
1960	327,172	21,284,084	−466,289	32.9
1961	318,359	20,308,444	−390,495	29.7
1962	313,084	19,926,466	−374,993	25.2
1963	310,999	18,519,049	−378,618	23.7
1964	314,386	18,271,322	−389,008	23.7
1965	305,822	17,161,776	−398,029	21.6
1966	307,530	17,162,776	−379,744	19.5
1967	304,028	15,264,172	−460,414	26.9
1968	301,372	13,163,541	−462,129	25.8
1969	301,673	12,213,983	−437,498	24.4
1970	289,469	10,785,746	−449,579	26.2

[a] The ICC did not separate passenger and freight net earnings before 1936.
SOURCES: Interstate Commerce Commission, *Statistics of Railways in the United States; Transport Statistics in the United States;* James C. Nelson, *Railroad Transportation and Public Policy* (Washington, D.C.: Brookings Institution, 1959).

to raise passenger volume during that period. Output apparently stabilized at about half the passenger-miles of 1920, but the passenger deficit also stabilized in the vicinity of $250 million per year.[3]

World War II brought the second major reversal in the secular decline of rail passenger traffic. Restrictions on commercial aviation and automobile travel at a time of high war-related demand for intercity transportation brought the number of passengers back to the level of the early 1920s and actually caused passenger-miles to reach double the 1920 level. In 1944 the railroads carried 916 million passengers for 95.7 billion passenger-miles. For four consecutive years, 1942 through 1945, the railroads had positive earnings from their passenger service.

[3] For time series of the railroads in this period, see James C. Nelson, *Railroad Transportation and Public Policy* (Washington, D.C.: Brookings Institution, 1959).

It would have been impossible for the railroads to maintain wartime levels of traffic, but there was initial optimism that providing the major trains with diesel locomotives and stainless steel or aluminum equipment would stabilize their volume at levels above those of the 1930s. But this was not to be: the passenger deficit reappeared in force and quickly made serious inroads into the industry's profitability. In 1949 the passenger deficit reached a record level of $650 million, almost half (48.6 percent) the railway net revenue from freight.

The situation was typical of regulated industries: the earnings from freight were expected to cross-subsidize passenger service. Generally, cross-subsidy is successful only in the short run. In the long run the discriminatory pricing structure it entails gives the economy an incentive to find alternatives to the regulated industries.[4] The railroad industry as a whole had been declining relative to trucking since at least 1916, but the regional pattern of the decline aggravated the difficulty of cross-subsidy. The remaining demand for railroad passenger service was highly concentrated east of Chicago and north of Washington, D.C., but the railroads in the Northeast were becoming the weakest in the country. The area was producing more services and fewer goods, and the goods it did produce were increasingly of a character appropriate to truck transport. The country was losing its comparative advantage for steel production, and coal was a declining industry. The Lehigh Valley, a former anthracite carrier, had lost most of its coal origination and was almost entirely dependent for freight traffic on a single steel plant in Bethlehem, Pennsylvania, but it retained a considerable absolute demand for passenger service. The New Haven had become almost exclusively an inbound terminating facility for freight, but it was the fourth largest passenger carrier in the industry.

The experience of the early 1950s was enough to disabuse an increasing percentage of railroad executives of any optimism remaining from the end of World War II. The reequipment of passenger trains in the late 1940s had not halted the decline. The passenger deficit was regularly over $500 million per year and dissipated more than 35 percent of net operating revenue from freight.

Apart from the wartime spurt, the railroads had actually conformed to the standard pattern of declining industries. That is, output had fallen at an increasing rate in the 1920s and at a decreasing rate thereafter. The virtually universal pattern is for the service to pass

---

[4] See Richard Posner, "Taxation by Regulation," *The Bell Journal of Economics and Management Science*, vol. 2 (1971), pp. 22–50.

out of existence after a long period of declining at a decreasing rate.[5] However, the decline of rail passenger service was protracted by restrictions on exit. Practically every state regulated the discontinuance of passenger trains, with little consistency overall. Mississippi's commission, lacking funds to administer the statute regulating discontinuance, simply allowed passenger trains to be withdrawn freely. The Maryland commission rarely objected to withdrawal of a passenger train. At the other extreme, North Dakota made it an explicit goal to retain the last local on branch lines in the state. Louisiana had elected commissioners, some of whom were pledged to their constituents to preserve passenger trains in the state.[6] Until 1958, the Interstate Commerce Commission (ICC) lacked the power to regulate discontinuance of passenger trains—the only major gap in the ICC's comprehensive regulatory power over the railroad industry.

The year 1958 was pivotal in three respects in the sequence of events leading to the establishment of the Amtrak system: the Transportation Act of 1958 vested the ICC with powers over discontinuance of passenger trains; the ICC received from its examiners' staff a major document on the railroad passenger deficit, the Hosmer Report; and, in the last few weeks of that year, jet aircraft were introduced into commercial intercity service in the United States.

The railroads had supported extending the ICC's powers to passenger train discontinuance, hoping that this body would be more consistent than were the various state commissions. The ICC's authority was contained in section 13a(1) and 13a(2) of the act, which conferred, respectively, original powers over the discontinuance of interstate trains and appellate powers over the discontinuance of intrastate trains that had been ordered continued by state authorities. The original draft of the act had provided that any demonstrably unprofitable passenger train might be discontinued, but New York Senator Jacob Javits, fearing that New York might shortly be denuded of its suburban services, removed this provision. The ICC, as a result, was given no specific directive but simply vested with a high degree of discretion. In exercise of this authority, the commission was to be faced continually with reasonably objective presentations of passenger trains' losses set against nebulous and subjective statements of their external benefits.[7]

---

[5] Hoffman, British Industry.

[6] George W. Hilton, The Transportation Act of 1958 (Bloomington, Ind.: Indiana University Press, 1969), pp. 35–36.

[7] For the statutory authority, see ibid., pp. 35–38; for experience under the act, see ibid., pp. 97–154.

Had the ICC seen fit to accept the 1958 report of Examiner Howard Hosmer and his staff, it would have had a source of unambiguous doctrine in these actions. The report, which the commission had initiated in 1956, dealt both with the accuracy of the passenger train deficit as annually reported and with its causes.[8] The techniques used to quantify the passenger deficit were typical of the ICC's accounting. Railroads were directed to report the variable cost of passenger train operation and to allocate the fixed cost of right-of-way between passenger and freight operations on the basis of relative train-miles. Inevitably, an average-cost computation of this character entails certain inaccuracies. It was generally accepted, for example, that little of the right-of-way cost of the Norfolk & Western and Chesapeake & Ohio, the two major coal carriers, could be attributed to their few passenger trains. On the other hand, the two largest passenger carriers, the Pennsylvania and New York Central, both considered the ICC's quantification close to accurate. Both had extensive four-track main lines on which about half the trains carried passengers, and both believed that in absence of passenger trains they could reduce the number of tracks to two. Thus, about half the fixed expense was, in fact, attributable to the passenger trains. The issue was a major one, because many proponents of rail passenger service argued that the passenger deficit was grossly overstated or, in extreme cases, that it was purely an accounting fiction. In 1957 the deficit reached $723 million, its historical high.

Examiner Hosmer considered the objections to the commission's methodology, but concluded that it produced a reasonably accurate figure. As recently as January 27, 1958, Division Two of the commission had reexamined the rules for allocating expenses between passenger and freight operations and concluded that they were "adequate for the purpose for which they are intended." Hosmer argued that the validity of the ICC formula had become essentially irrelevant. American passenger trains in the aggregate had last covered their variable expenses in 1952. By 1957, the costs related solely to passenger service were alone producing a deficit of $114 million per year. Hosmer also took note of a recent study, *Avoidable Costs of Passenger Train Service* by the Aeronautical Research Foundation, which con-

---

[8] *Railroad Passenger Train Deficit*, report proposed by Howard Hosmer, hearing examiner, assisted by Robert A. Berrien, Fred A. Christoph, and Raymond C. Smith, attorney advisers, Docket no. 31954 (1958), hereafter cited as Hosmer Report. For an appreciation of the economic content of the report, see George W. Hilton, "The Hosmer Report: A Decennial Evaluation," *ICC Practitioners' Journal*, vol. 36 (1969), pp. 1470–1486.

cluded that the ICC formula systematically understated the deficit by neglecting the cost of having freight trains wait in sidings and other opportunity costs of passenger-train interference with freight operations.

Hosmer then proceeded to an economic (demand and supply) analysis of the causes of the deficit. He attributed the decline in demand for passenger service to the traveling public's increased preference for highway and air transportation. On the supply side, he found an extreme labor-intensiveness that gave the passenger train a higher rate of increase in costs than rival carriers. He also demonstrated that operating rules were more suitable to railroad freight operations than to passenger service.

Examiner Hosmer then proceeded to consider possible remedies for the passenger deficit. On the basis of experience with ICC-mandated fare reductions in 1936, he concluded that fare policy was unlikely to arrest the diversion of riders. He noted that neither the luxury equipment installed between 1946 and 1951 nor the spartan lightweight equipment which had a brief vogue in 1954 had succeeded in retaining passengers. Neither cheaper dining arrangements nor agreement for cost reduction with the railroad brotherhoods appeared promising as a cost-saving device. Hosmer said explicitly that a public subsidy for rail passenger service was unlikely to be successful because of the federal government's heavy annual expenditures on highways and air facilities.

Finally, Hosmer necessarily considered the passenger train problem in light of the National Transportation Policy of 1940, the preamble to the Interstate Commerce Act, which was intended by Congress to be the ICC's basic directive. This policy directed the ICC to produce a transportation system adequate to the needs of commerce, the postal service, and the national defense. With respect to the needs of commerce, Hosmer demonstrated that the passenger train held such a small share of the intercity travel market that it no longer served a significant demand. Instead, it produced deficits that promised to impede the railroads' ability to serve other demands in the economy. Second, he pointed out that the U.S. Post Office was accelerating its diversion of first-class mail to air carriers and that the postal authorities envisioned shipping other forms of mail by rail in containers or in other fashions unrelated to the passenger train. Finally, although he did not deny that the railroads might again move troops in massive numbers as they had in World War II, Hosmer held that preparing for such an emergency was a problem for the defense establishment, not for a regulatory commission.

The Hosmer Report concluded, inevitably, that the passenger train was hopeless and would shortly pass out of existence:

> For more than a century the railroad passenger coach has occupied an interesting and useful place in American life, but at the present time the inescapable fact—and certainly to many people an unpleasant one—seems to be that in a decade or so this time-honored vehicle may take its place in the transportation museum along with the stagecoach, the side-wheeler, and the steam locomotive. It is repetitious to add that this outcome will be due to the fact that the American public now is doing about ninety percent of its travelling by private automobile and prefers to do so. The percentage of travel by public carriers is bound to diminish as more highways continue to be built.
>
> The railroads' share of the ten percent of total travel by public carriers is roughly thirty percent thereof compared with a combined percentage of about forty percent for air and bus. The railroad percentage seems certain to shrink when the new jet transports, capable of flying from coast to coast in less than five hours, are placed in service.
>
> If railroad passenger-miles (other than commutation) continue to decline at the average rate of reduction between 1947 and 1957, the parlor and sleeping-car service will have disappeared by 1965 and the coach service by 1970.[9]

In the course of his conclusion, Hosmer made a particularly direct attack on the argument that the decline of the passenger train was a product of the railroads' indifference or hostility to passenger traffic. In fact, he noted that the railroads had made an exceptional effort to preserve passenger service, partly because of their legal obligations, partly from a sense of public responsibility, and partly out of a long tradition in the industry. The report's final observation was:

> The passenger deficit is not something which can be conjured away by statistical legerdemain. It is real and serious. Unless a good start toward reducing it can be promptly made, the future of the railroads will be gravely endangered. In fact, there is here a disturbing overtone due to an implication that the passenger deficit may be a symptom of more deep-seated infirmities for which some remedy must be found if the railroads are to survive.[10]

The Hosmer Report, though written by a lawyer, was an excellent piece of economic analysis by the usual standards of evaluation:

[9] Hosmer Report, p. 69.
[10] Ibid., p. 72.

internal consistency of the argument, external consistency with the supporting evidence, consistency with what economists were producing in the same period regarding the passenger train, and, most important, predictive ability. Economists produced several estimates of income elasticity of demand for the various forms of passenger transportation around the time of the Hosmer Report. In 1955 Lewis J. Paradiso and Clement Wilson estimated the income elasticity of demand for intercity rail passenger service at −0.6, which is to say that an American family would respond to a 1 percent increase in income by demanding 0.6 percent less intercity rail passenger service.[11] Estimates by Walter Oi, Norman Asher, and their collaborators in the 1960s for rival carriers were +1.2 for the automobile and +2.5 for commercial air transportation.[12] Introduction of the jet transport late in 1958 greatly increased the comfort, speed, and safety of air transport, thereby probably rendering the income elasticity of demand for rail transport even more unfavorable than it was in 1955 when Paradiso and Wilson published their estimate.

The relative income elasticities of demand for the major forms of intercity passenger transport implied that the demand for luxury rail travel—Pullman service, dining car meals, and club car facilities—would decline faster than the demand for basic coach service. Examiner Hosmer noted this in his extrapolation that Pullman service would terminate some five years before coach service. The luxury services were also the most labor-intensive portion of rail passenger service. Accordingly, on all grounds, railroads had greater incentive to terminate them than to wind up the passenger train completely.

For most passengers it would have been inconsistent to demand a high standard of comfort while spending forty hours to save twenty dollars, as a passenger did in choosing rail over air for the trip from Chicago to Los Angeles in 1958. However, there were two major exceptions: the affluent elderly with a low valuation of time and enthusiasts who rode railroads for pleasure would both be consistent in preferring high standards of service. To many—but not all—of these two groups and to many other individuals, the withdrawal of Pullman cars, the replacement of dining cars with automatic vending equipment, and other adaptations by the railroads to the declining demand for luxury service appeared to be efforts to discourage the

---

[11] "Consumer Expenditure-Income Patterns," *Survey of Current Business*, vol. 25 (September 1955), p. 29.
[12] Walter Oi and Paul W. Shuldiner, *An Analysis of Urban Travel Demands* (Evanston, Ill.: Northwestern University Press, 1962), p. 182; Norman Asher et al., *Demand Analysis for Air Travel by Supersonic Transport* (Washington, D.C.: Institute for Defense Analysis, 1966), Report no. R–118, vol. 1, p. 8.

use of passenger trains. The Hosmer Report explicitly showed this interpretation to be false, but it remained widespread. The most extreme statement of it, Peter Lyon's *To Hell in a Day Coach*, argued that the passenger deficit was entirely a fiction—that railroads discouraged passenger service simply because freight was more profitable and because freight was either inanimate or inarticulate so that it could not complain about habitual standards of rail service. Nonetheless, he considered trains either actually or potentially the most satisfactory form of intercity passenger transport and proposed nationalizing the intercity passenger train system.[13] The logic of the discouragement hypothesis implied that under a nationalized system, the incentives of the managers would be toward improving the quality of service and thereby reversing the decline of the passenger train.

Actually, a study by the Stanford Research Institute, commissioned by the Southern Pacific, had demonstrated that railroads which attempted to maintain traditional standards of passenger service—the Santa Fe, Great Northern, Northern Pacific, Burlington Route—had merely damped the rate of decline at the cost of considerable increase in their passenger deficits relative to other railroads, such as the Southern Pacific, which had responded to the demand conditions.[14] The study also contained a cost comparison that was consistent with the Hosmer Report's conclusion adverse to the passenger train. The Stanford Research Institute's economists found that it cost the Southern Pacific $18.41 to move a coach passenger between San Francisco and Los Angeles on its *Coast Daylight*. Air carriers on the same route could move a passenger in a Boeing 727 for $9.89, and Western Greyhound Lines could do it for $9.11.

The cost disadvantage was not only in the labor-intensiveness of the trains, which required approximately sixteen employees for a one-way trip, but also in the low utilization rate of equipment. The train and a Boeing 727, as of about 1965, each represented an investment of about $3.6 million. The train could produce one one-way trip per day; the plane, with a single crew of seven, could produce two round trips per day. With a second crew, it could double that output.[15] With the introduction of larger aircraft in the late 1960s the productivity of aircraft increased. A single stretched DC-8 of 250-passenger capacity assigned to a long-distance route, such as Atlanta—Los Angeles, could turn in more passenger-miles per year than the entire

---

[13] Peter Lyon, *To Hell in a Day Coach* (New York: Lippincott, 1968).

[14] Ely M. Brandes and Alan E. Lazar, *Rail Passenger Traffic in the West* (Menlo Park, Calif.: Stanford Research Institute, 1966), pp. 19–30.

[15] Ibid., pp. 8–10.

Atlantic Coast Line Railroad, the dominant railroad in East Coast—Florida passenger operations.[16]

The academic studies mentioned above, appearing just before and just after the Hosmer Report, were consistent with it and lent strength to its conclusion. They suggest strongly that the ICC should have been guided in its control of passenger train discontinuance by Examiner Hosmer's recommendation. Instead, however, the commission concluded in the decision that presented most of the empirical content of the Hosmer Report: "We are of the view that the complete elimination of passenger train service would not be a solution in the public interest. Economic railroad passenger service is, and for the foreseeable future will be, an integral part of the national transportation system, and essential for the nation's well-being and defense."[17]

On the other hand, the ICC was constrained by considerations of confiscation of the property of a regulated firm not to require indefinite cross-subsidy of an unprofitable train. By analogy to its longstanding doctrine with respect to branch-line abandonments, the commission early on held that it would not require indefinite perpetuation of an otherwise unprofitable passenger train on the ground that the railroad as a whole was profitable.[18]

These two doctrines were inconsistent. As the Hosmer Report demonstrated, the forces causing the decline in demand for and the increase in costs of rail passenger service were such that any individual train, even if currently profitable, would inevitably become chronically unprofitable. The contradiction was convenient, however, because the commission could bring forth either doctrine as required in any specific case. And in fact, it alternated between the two.[19] The rate of withdrawal of passenger trains did increase after 1958.[20] The introduction of jet aircraft, as Hosmer had anticipated, accelerated the decline in demand for rail passenger service, and introduction of the zip code system in 1963 resulted in an accelerated withdrawal of mail.

The passenger train declined as one might have expected: the local trains were largely withdrawn in the 1920s, and secondary main line trains followed in the 1930s, 1940s, and 1950s. By 1967, the remaining major trains were threatened, but the ICC at this time began to toughen its criteria for discontinuance of trains in the basic network.

---

[16] See Delta Air Line advertisement, *Air Travel*, July 1967, following p. 54.

[17] Railroad Passenger Train Deficit, Docket no. 31954, p. 103.

[18] Great Northern Ry. Co. Discontinuance of Service, Williston, N.D., Watford City, N. D., and Richey, Mont., 307 ICC 59 (1959) at 69.

[19] Hilton, *Transportation Act of 1958*, pp. 97–154.

[20] Ibid., p. 135.

With the notable exception of the last remaining Chicago-Atlanta train, it managed to preserve at least one train on every major long-distance route. Beginning in June 1968, the commission advocated a bill, S. 3861–H.R. 18212, providing more rigorous legislative standards for train discontinuance, longer time periods for ICC consideration of such actions, exclusive jurisdiction to the ICC over discontinuance of the last train on any route, and finally, study by the Department of Transportation in collaboration with the ICC on "financing operations which are necessary but not economically viable."[21]

The end of the passenger train was clearly at hand. The number of trains, which had reached 20,000 in 1929, was down to 500, and over 100 of these were the subject of discontinuance proceedings. The commission complained that it was increasingly difficult to require continuance without placing an undue burden on interstate commerce.

In 1967 Anthony Haswell founded the National Association of Railroad Passengers, a lobbying organization for the preservation and upgrading of passenger trains. While employed as a lawyer in the legal department of the Illinois Central Railroad, Haswell had become persuaded of the discouragement hypothesis of the passenger train's decline. He expressed in a television interview the opinion that upgrading the quality of service could restore volume to approximately 1950 levels.[22]

Because the remaining passenger train network served every major region in the United States, preservation of the passenger train had wide geographic support that was reflected particularly strongly in the House of Representatives. Sentiment was divided between direct federal subsidy to individual railroads and creation of a federal corporation to operate the trains. The preference of Secretary of Transportation John A. Volpe for a federal corporation tipped the balance in that direction. The National Railroad Passenger Corporation was established under the Rail Passenger Service Act of 1970, which was passed by the Senate on May 6 and by the House on October 14 of that year.[23] The Office of Management and Budget reportedly considered preservation of the passenger train hopeless and recommended that President Richard Nixon veto the bill. He was widely expected to do so until very shortly before his decision had to be made. He determined to sign the bill, however, and it became law on October 30, 1970.

---

[21] Ibid., pp. 153–154.
[22] Telecast, confirmed by letter of Anthony Haswell, August 8, 1978.
[23] Public Law 91–518.

2
Amtrak's Statutory Authority and Planning Procedures

The Rail Passenger Service Act of 1970[1] established the National Railroad Passenger Corporation as a for-profit enterprise, incorporated under the District of Columbia Business Corporation Act. The act is thus consistent with the discouragement hypothesis of the decline of the passenger train in that it recognized no reason why the operation should not be profitable with a new incentive structure. The firm was to be formed by three or more incorporators appointed by the president. Thereafter, it was to have fifteen directors (including a chairman), eight appointed by the president with the approval of the Senate, three elected by the common stockholders, and four elected by the preferred stockholders. Common stock was to be issued only to railroads, whereas preferred stock was to be held by investors other than railroads or entities that controlled railroads.

Railroads could become stockholders by paying in an amount computed by one of three formulas, whichever was most favorable to the railroad: (1) 50 percent of the fully allocated passenger deficits of the railroad for 1969; (2) 100 percent of the avoidable loss for all intercity rail passenger service operated by the railroad during 1969; (3) 200 percent of the avoidable loss for the intercity rail passenger service operated in 1969 by the railroad over routes between points chosen for the basic system, as determined by the corporation's planning procedures. The amount was to be paid in by the railroad either in cash, in equipment, or in obligations to provide future service. Alternatively, a railroad might waive its right to receive stock and simply write off its contribution as a tax loss. Only four railroads chose to become stockholders: the Burlington Northern, Grand Trunk

---

[1] Public Law 91–518.

Western, Milwaukee Road, and Penn Central. The Burlington Northern was a solvent railroad, but the others all had long histories of deficits such that an additional tax write-off was not marginally attractive. All the other railroads that joined the system preferred the write-offs. The preferred stock was never issued.

Railroads had free choice whether to join the system. If they did join, they were relieved of all further obligation to operate intercity passenger trains after the date of the corporation's beginning operation, originally March 1, 1971, but postponed to May 1, 1971. Railroads that chose not to join the system were denied the right to discontinue passenger trains under section 13a(1) and 13a(2) of the Interstate Commerce Act until January 1, 1975. These terms persuaded most railroads to join.

The principal railroad to decide against joining was the Southern Railway. Its management felt that the terms made it a matter of indifference whether to participate or to continue running its four remaining passenger trains. The Denver & Rio Grande Western, which operated a single passenger train the length of its main line three days per week, remained outside because it expected the new corporation to run a daily Chicago-Oakland train over that line, and it was unwilling to experience greater interference with its freight trains. The Chicago, Rock Island & Pacific, a very weak large railroad, operated single trains from Chicago to Peoria and Rock Island. The railroad correctly anticipated that the state of Illinois would subsidize the operation. The Georgia Railroad enjoyed a tax remission for providing mixed train service over its entire system and feared withdrawal of the tax benefit. The Reading Company interpreted its remaining passenger service as commutation not covered by the statute but subject to local subsidies in its area.

Most of the railroads that joined the system paid their subscriptions in the form of equipment. The corporation's initial stock of equipment was 1,200 cars acquired from nine railroads for $16.8 million. Of these cars 90 percent were stainless steel with a modal age of twenty-one years. The equipment was highly depreciated: the average new value of the cars was about $100,000, but the cost of acquisition was about $14,000 and the scrap value about $2,000.[2] From the Santa Fe system the corporation bought 447 cars including 73 high-level coaches, diners, and lounges that were only ten years old. From the Union Pacific, the corporation bought 64 coaches, half of them completed in 1965. These two acquisitions gave the corporation

---

[2] *Trains*, November 1971, p. 4.

a supply of relatively modern rolling stock in good condition for basic main line services.[3] The corporation also acquired 61 multiple-unit, high-speed electric cars—the Metroliners that were built after 1965 under a federal program for upgrading rail passenger service in the northeast corridor.

It should be noted that the standard equipment acquired by the corporation was fitted with the usual system of steam heating and cooling. This technology, which dated from the days of the steam locomotive, had been perpetuated by the railroads' usual problem with major changes in technology: they require a communal decision. The system had the advantage of being compatible from one railroad to the next, but it was highly susceptible to malfunction. The jarring of steel wheels on steel rails frequently caused the system to overheat or underheat cars, and the technology was particularly prone to freezing in subzero cold. Excessive or inadequate heat had been the railroads' principal complaint from passengers, and the new corporation was to have the same experience. Consequently, since the new policy sought to reverse the decline of the passenger train through increasing the quality of service, the corporation found itself continually preoccupied with finding an alternative to steam heating and cooling.

It was originally anticipated that the corporation would operate under the trade name Railpax. Apparently because this word is too easily corrupted, the corporation chose instead the name Amtrak, a contraction of "American travel by track." The corporation adopted as its logo a headless arrow in red, white, and blue. The headless arrow and the word "Amtrak" in sans-serif lettering became the corporation's universal identification.

Congress provided Amtrak with an outright grant of $40 million to begin operations. The railroads' entry fees into the system totaled $197 million, payable in monthly installments over three years. Congress authorized Amtrak to issue guaranteed loans of $100 million.

The act required Amtrak to establish a basic rail system through a multistage planning process. The corporation was allowed to provide service in excess of the basic system if consistent with prudent management. In a provision that was to prove major, section 403(b), Amtrak was also empowered to provide additional service for any state, local, or regional government body willing to bear two-thirds of the losses.

---

[3] On the original rolling stock, see Fred W. Frailey, *Zephyrs, Chiefs, and Other Orphans: The First Five Years of Amtrak* (Godfrey, Ill.: RPC Publications, 1977).

The Initial Planning Operation

The 1970 act directed the secretary of transportation to initiate the planning operation by designating the end points in a basic system of intercity rail transport. On November 30, 1970, Secretary John A. Volpe issued a preliminary report to Congress and the Interstate Commerce Commission containing his recommendations. The report was submitted for comment to state regulatory commissions, the railroads, railway labor organizations, the National Association of Railroad Passengers, and the public at large. The secretary's proposal is most easily described as sets of radial routes from Chicago and New York. From Chicago trains were to run to Seattle, San Francisco, Los Angeles, Houston, St. Louis, New Orleans, Miami, Cincinnati, Detroit, and New York. From New York trains were to run to Buffalo, Boston, Washington, New Orleans, and Miami. One additional route was provided, Washington to St. Louis.[4]

The proposed radial pattern was met immediately with two antithetical criticisms. Some of the advocates of the program believed that the passenger train's comparative advantage was for medium-distance corridor services such as Chicago–Detroit, Chicago–St. Louis, New York–Buffalo, and the eastern seaboard high-speed line. These observers felt that Amtrak would be wasting its resources on transcontinental trains from Chicago to the West Coast, which were intrinsically hopeless. The opposite criticism was that the radial pattern fell short of providing a full nationwide system of passenger trains. Specifically, the radial pattern provided no service north and south along the West Coast and no service from Los Angeles to the South. Proponents of the latter position were successful. Secretary Volpe's final report, issued on January 28, 1971, added routes between Seattle and San Diego, Los Angeles and New Orleans, and Norfolk and Cincinnati. A St. Louis–Kansas City route was added as an extension of the service from the East Coast to St. Louis.[5]

The eight incorporators of the corporation were then required to choose specific routes between the twenty-one pairs of cities that the secretary had chosen for the nationwide system. Their decisions were based on the following criteria: (1) current train ridership and number of trains per week; (2) current operating costs on each route; (3) adequacy of other travel modes; (4) total population of cities along the route; and (5) physical characteristics of track and equipment. These criteria led to certain obvious choices: the Santa Fe main line

---

[4] *Trains*, March 1971, p. 3.
[5] *Trains*, April 1971, pp. 4, 6.

from Chicago to Los Angeles; the Illinois Central from Chicago to New Orleans; the Southern Pacific and connections from Seattle and Portland to Los Angeles and San Diego; and both Seaboard Coast Line main lines between Washington, D.C., and Florida.

The Santa Fe line through Kansas City and Wichita was chosen as the route to Ft. Worth and Houston in preference to the Missouri Pacific main line through Little Rock. The train from Chicago to Florida points was routed through Indianapolis, Louisville, Nashville, and Birmingham rather than duplicating the route of the Illinois Central Railroad's *City of Miami*, a train that was still covering its variable costs. Similarly, Amtrak avoided a route through Atlanta, the largest intermediate city. The Southern Railway's failure to join relieved Amtrak of the obligation to provide a train between Washington, D.C., and New Orleans via Atlanta. The Southern Railway continued its existing train, the *Southern Crescent*, over that route. The Denver & Rio Grande Western's failure to join the system prevented Amtrak from operating its Chicago–Oakland train via Grand Junction and Salt Lake City. Rather, it chose the Union Pacific line between Denver and Ogden, Utah.

The most surprising choice was the former Great Northern Railway main line of the Burlington Northern across North Dakota and Montana. The choice was reportedly dictated by the virtual absence of rival modes of public transportation through that lightly populated area. However, most of the population of Montana was located on the former Northern Pacific main line of the Burlington Northern. The incorporators' choice was unsatisfactory to the two senators from Montana, one of whom was the Senate majority leader and the other a long-time advocate of passenger train preservation. The two successfully led efforts to have Amtrak add a train three times per week over the former Northern Pacific main line.

Similar evidence of political resource allocation abounded throughout the system. Senators from Indiana had interested themselves in transportation policy, whereas senators and representatives from Ohio generally had not. Indianapolis was served by three Amtrak routes, but Cleveland initially by none at all. West Virginia was the home state of the chairman of the House Commerce Committee, a prominent member of the ICC, and a senator who was to become majority leader. The initial plan called for a passenger train on the Chesapeake & Ohio main line, but another was added between Washington and Parkersburg, West Virginia, along the Baltimore & Ohio's St. Louis line. Establishing service in the absence of effective demand could readily be justified on the criterion of inadequacy of rival public transportation. By 1972, Amtrak was running trains from Chicago seven times weekly to Los Angeles, an SMSA (standard metropolitan statistical area) of 8 million people, and seven times weekly to the San Francisco Bay area, SMSA population 4 million, but ten times weekly to Seattle-Tacoma, an SMSA of only 2 million people.[6] Besides the political pressures of the Montana senators, Seattle also benefited from activities of a senator and a representative from Washington, both of whom had particularly identified themselves with transportation policy.

Thus, even within the constraints provided, the system was not optimal for serving the remaining demand. Because most routes were served by a single train per day, maintenance facilities would have to be widely dispersed, lightly utilized, and, consequently, very expensive. The transcontinental service could probably have been provided more cheaply by a single train on the Union Pacific main line dividing at Ogden, Utah, for service to Seattle-Portland, the San Francisco Bay area, and southern California along the lines of the Union Pacific's previous practice. However, the political element in the planning process and its wasteful consequences were inevitable. In establishing Amtrak, Congress had decided on political resource allocation because market allocation was about to eliminate rail passenger service. There was nothing in the statutory authority to assure optimality in the second-best sense of optimizing within undesirable constraints.

Amtrak was empowered either to operate trains directly or to contract with the railroads for the service. Inevitably, the corporation began by contracting with the railroads. Amtrak's payments were to be the avoidable costs, that is, the out-of-pocket costs related solely to passenger service, plus 5 percent to compensate the railroad for joint costs such as maintenance-of-way, operation of interlockings, delay of freight trains, and other costs not readily identifiable as passenger-related. Cost-plus contracting, as the defense industry's experience had amply demonstrated, provides inadequate incentive to hold down costs.

Only the Penn Central was to challenge the adequacy of the 5 percent compensation for joint costs. Judge John P. Fullam, who was responsible for the affairs of the bankrupt Penn Central, had approved the arrangement on April 28, 1971, but the railroad later brought the issue before the ICC. On September 24, 1973, the commission required Amtrak to pay rent on the Penn Central's Boston–New York–Washington facilities, on which Amtrak ran approximately

---

[6] 1970 SMSA populations, *World Almanac*, 1979, p. 210.

40 percent of the trains by a complicated formula. The rental was computed on the basis of fully allocated costs plus a 7.5 percent return on investment, measured as 39.7 percent of the historical cost less recorded depreciation on the trackage. For use of other Penn Central facilities, Amtrak was ordered to pay on the basis of an avoidable cost formula with no return on investment. The commission reasoned that a large portion of the investment on the East Coast corridor existed because of the trains Amtrak ran, whereas Penn Central facilities elsewhere would be essentially the same if Amtrak were not operating there.[7] The decision was expected to increase Amtrak's yearly payment to the Penn Central from $40 million to $80 or $100 million.[8] Simultaneously, the ICC approved Amtrak's request that five incentives be built into the Penn Central's contract: schedule adherence, excessive delay, schedule improvement, cleanliness, and equipment operability. An incentive contract was developed by Professor William J. Baumol of Princeton University and his associates.[9]

Revisions in the Statutory Authority

When Amtrak proved in short order to be more unprofitable than anticipated, Congress responded readily with additional funds, once with even more than Amtrak had requested. The National Passenger Corporation Assistance Act, the appropriation bill enacted June 22, 1972, made some minor changes in Amtrak's statutory authority.[10] The act has usually been interpreted as a vote of confidence in the Amtrak concept but lack of confidence in the initial management. Congress directed Amtrak to assume operation of trains insofar as possible and to endeavor to increase mail and express revenue. The act authorized the Department of Transportation to grant up to $225 million for maintenance, repairs, research and development, and for demonstration and capital improvements.

The act specifically provided subsidies for three international routes, which became the *Inter-American* from St. Louis to Nuevo Laredo, Mexico, via Little Rock; the *Pacific International* between Seattle and Vancouver; and the *Montrealer* between Washington, D.C.,

---

[7] George P. Baker, Richard C. Bond and Jervis Langdon, Jr., Trustees of the Penn Central Transportation Co., Debtor—Compensation for Passenger Service, F.D. 27353 (1973).

[8] *Trains*, December 1973, pp. 10–12.

[9] William J. Baumol, "Payment by Performance in Rail Passenger Transportation: An Innovation in Amtrak's Operations," *The Bell Journal of Economics*, vol. 6 (1975), pp. 281–298.

[10] Public Law 92–316.

and Montreal. The *Montrealer* and *Inter-American* were revivals of services that had been discontinued before Amtrak's establishment. The act designated the three routes as part of Amtrak's basic system, not requiring state subsidy and subject to ICC jurisdiction over discontinuance. The *Montrealer* required operation over the Boston & Maine, Central Vermont, and Canadian National, railroads that had not participated in Amtrak at the outset.

The act directed Amtrak to provide special fares for military personnel and blind persons and directed the federal government to authorize train travel on the same basis as other modes. It also provided for monthly reports to Congress on revenues, expenses, loads, and punctuality, plus annual reports to the ICC and the Department of Transportation. The ICC was required to rule within ninety days on Amtrak's applications for use of railroad tracks and facilities. The criteria for granting additional routes were to be population, alternative forms of transportation, economic conditions, and costs. People who had been entitled to passes on April 30, 1971, were granted reduced fares on Amtrak. The House appended a requirement that the secretary of transportation include in his annual recommendations for legislative action comments on discontinuance, development, expansion, or contraction in the Amtrak system.

The recommendations required by the new statute appeared on March 15, 1973.[11] The secretary's report was generally favorable to the Amtrak experiment but suggested discontinuance of the Washington–Parkersburg train, the *Floridian* between Chicago and Miami, and the Newport News–Charlottesville connection to the train on the Chesapeake & Ohio main line. The Parkersburg train was cut back to Cumberland, Maryland, in May 1973. Amtrak filed to discontinue the Newport News train, but was rejected by the ICC on the ground that the train was intrastate. The department also proposed moving back the terminus of the *National Limited* from St. Louis to Pittsburgh, and that of the *Texas Chief* from Chicago to Newton, Kansas. Amtrak filed to discontinue the *Floridian* and the west end of the *National Limited*, but withdrew the applications in the face of congressional pressure. The secretary's report also recommended eliminating the ICC's authority over Amtrak. The commission had had from the outset the odd combination of authority over Amtrak's discontinuances and its quality of service and no authority over its rates.

Congress moved instead in the opposite direction. In a second and more important amendment to the statutory authority, the Amtrak

---

11 "Report to Congress on the Rail Passenger Service Act," submitted by the secretary of transportation, March 15, 1973.

Improvement Act of 1973,[12] Congress attempted to make Amtrak permanent, to make discontinuances more difficult, and to assure expansion of the system. Further, Congress placed two additional representatives of consumer groups on Amtrak's Board of Directors and restricted the voting rights of directors representing the railroads in cases of conflict of interest.

The new act rescinded the original statute's requirement that Amtrak depend on the railroads for employees. The change was consistent with the original act's intention of providing institutional arrangements that fostered a single-valued incentive to make rail passenger service succeed.

The act contained several provisions concerning operation of rail auto-ferry services. It confirmed Amtrak's authority to run auto-ferry services like that operated by Auto-Train. The law also empowered any person or corporation, except a railroad participating in Amtrak, to operate such services by securing a certificate of public convenience and necessity from the ICC. This had the effect of closing entry into the auto-ferry business. Amtrak, even though it was then trying to remove the *Floridian*, had sought to prevent Auto-Train from establishing an auto-ferry between Louisville and Sanford, Florida. Amtrak sought to restrict Auto-Train to its original route, but Auto-Train successfully contended that its contract with the Family Lines included the entire system of the Seaboard Coast Line, Louisville & Nashville, and affiliates. The company then instituted the Louisville–Sanford train. On May 1, 1974, Amtrak made a test run of an Indianapolis–Kissimmee, Florida, auto-ferry called *Auto-Trak*, but the run produced a large damage claim from the Avis automobiles aboard. Amtrak then decided against the service.[13]

The act also prohibited a railroad from invoking state law to support its refusal to participate with Amtrak in establishing an auto-ferry. The Southern Pacific had refused to operate an Oakland–Portland auto-ferry on the ground that California state law prohibited operation of mixed trains. The state law was subsequently repealed, but the service was never inaugurated.[14]

The act of 1973 also provided for assurance of access to Amtrak facilities for the elderly and the handicapped. It further granted Amtrak the right of eminent domain and empowered it to condemn property.

---

[12] Public Law 93–146.
[13] *Trains*, January 1975, pp. 6–7.
[14] Ibid.

The act required Amtrak to pay subcontractors' costs above the level that would exist in its absence, as distinct from paying prorated joint costs as the Penn Central had requested. The law further provided for bonuses above the level of avoidable cost for performance. This provision underlay an ICC decision that greatly increased Amtrak's cost of operation. The Texas & Pacific Railway successfully contended that it was maintaining its track on a higher level than it would have otherwise because Amtrak's *Inter-American* was using it. The ICC ordered Amtrak to reimburse the railroad for its higher track maintenance costs even though Amtrak believed the additional costs were unjustified.[15] Amtrak estimated that the decision would increase its operating costs about $1.30 per train-mile, or $80–100 million annually. Previously, the Association of American Railroads had estimated that the twelve principal railroads subcontracting with Amtrak were subsidizing it by about $52 million per year because of noncompensatory fees.[16] After the ICC decision, the association found Amtrak's fees to be entirely compensatory except possibly for certain costs in the delay of freight trains.[17]

The 1973 act required that Amtrak trains be given priority over freight trains except where the secretary of transportation waived the priority. The secretary was also empowered to rule on Amtrak's requests for higher speed limits.

Amtrak had been directed initially to operate its basic system without change (that is, discontinuances) until 1973. In this statute Congress extended that date to July 1, 1974. Congress also required Amtrak to add an experimental route each year to be operated for at least three years. Any experimental services inaugurated by Amtrak on its own initiative were not to be discontinued before November 1974.

The act prohibited the White House or the Department of Transportation from demanding information from Amtrak prior to its being submitted to Congress. This was an effort to reduce the power of the Office of Management and Budget over Amtrak and to reduce the authority of the Department of Transportation on Amtrak's board. This provision caused Secretary of Transportation Claude Brinegar to urge President Nixon to veto the act, but he did not do so. The Budget

---

[15] National Railroad Passenger Corporation and the Texas & Pacific Ry. Co., Use of Tracks and Facilities and Establishing Just Compensation, 348 ICC 357 (1975); Amtrak and the Texas & Pacific Ry. Co., Use of Tracks and Facilities and Establishment of Just Compensation, 348 ICC 645 (1976).

[16] *Trains*, August 1973, p. 6.

[17] Interview with James McClellan, Association of American Railroads, June 23, 1977.

24

and Impoundment Control Act of 1974 was a further effort by Congress to protect Amtrak from hostility in the executive branch. This statute gave either house the right to veto presidential impoundment of funds, a practice that had impeded Amtrak previously.

The original act gave the ICC jurisdiction over the quality of rail passenger service, a power the commission had previously ruled that it lacked.[18] The 1973 act required the commission to produce its rules on this topic by January 2, 1974. On December 27, 1973, the ICC issued *Ex Parte No. 277*, effective April 1, 1974, setting forth rules for the behavior of Amtrak and any railroad that provided over 500 passenger train–miles per day.[19] Commuter and mixed trains were apparently exempt. In addition, a carrier might petition for exemption from any of the rules. The principal requirements were, first, the provision of a toll-free telephone reservation system in which reservations were confirmed within an hour and held for the passenger up to thirty minutes before departure. Amtrak petitioned that the reservations be paid for and tickets picked up twenty-four hours in advance of departure, but subsequently amended the petition to one hour before departure. The second requirement was that trains arrive within five minutes of scheduled time per 100 miles of travel, or thirty minutes, whichever was less. Priority of passenger trains over freight trains was again demanded. Third, patrolled stations were required to be open for a sufficient time before and after trains for boarding of passengers and delivery of checked baggage within thirty minutes of arrival. Fourth, the rules required carriers to provide sufficient equipment to protect peak loads of traffic, to provide assistance for the elderly and handicapped, and to check baggage on trains with runs of over 200 miles.

Finally, the ICC included a required list of amenities. Carriers must provide food and beverage service on all trains operating over two hours, full diners on runs of over twelve hours, private-room sleeping cars on trains operating six hours or more between midnight and 8:00 A.M., and economy-type sleeping cars on such trains to the extent practical. Reclining-seat, leg-rest coaches with clean pillows were required on trains operating four hours or more between 10:00 P.M. and 8:00 A.M. Nonrevenue lounge space was required for runs of six hours or more, and at least one dome car was required on trains operating sixteen hours or more, if clearances permitted. The

---

[18] Adequacies—Passenger Service, Southern Pacific Co., between California and Louisiana, 335 ICC 415 (1969).

[19] Ex Parte No. 277, Adequacy of Intercity Rail Passenger Service, 351 ICC 883 (1976).

carriers had to maintain temperatures between 60 and 80 degrees and separate smokers and nonsmokers. Compliance was to be to the maximum extent feasible in recognition of poor track and various other handicaps under which Amtrak operated. The regulations provided for fines of up to $500 per unresolved violation.

The deterioration of the northeastern railroads, in particular, was to impede Amtrak considerably. Under the 1973 act, Secretary Brinegar in June 1974 ordered restoration of the *Lake Shore Limited*, a train on the former New York Central main line between New York and Chicago via Cleveland. However, because of a shortage of equipment and the removal of twelve miles of track near Albany, it proved impossible to reestablish the train.[20] Simultaneously, Brinegar directed Amtrak to establish a route from Washington to Denver via the Baltimore & Ohio to Cincinnati, the Penn Central to Indianapolis and St. Louis, the Missouri Pacific to Kansas City, and the Santa Fe to Denver. This proved impossible because of the deteriorated condition of the Penn Central west of Cincinnati. The train was restored only as a Washington–Cincinnati train, essentially an extended version of the Washington–Parkersburg train previously discontinued.[21]

The third revision of Amtrak's statutory authority was the Amtrak Improvement Act of 1974,[22] signed by President Gerald Ford in October of that year. This statute provided $200 million for operations for the fiscal year, more than had been requested. The act also expanded the volume of guaranteed loans available to Amtrak to $900 million. Further expansion of the system was required, beginning with a route from Ogden, Utah, to Portland, Oregon, via Boise, Idaho.

Amtrak's chronic unprofitability created a need for annual legislation to pay its losses. The next statute again postponed the dates for discontinuances from Amtrak's basic network, this time to October 1, 1976, and for services established by Amtrak after January 1, 1973, to March 1, 1977. It specifically provided that the Oakland–Bakersfield and the stillborn Washington–Denver trains not be discontinued before March 1, 1977. The act directed Amtrak to present Congress with criteria and procedures for discontinuance of trains. If Congress approved the criteria, Amtrak would be able in the future to discontinue services without the approval of the ICC.

The act passed in May 1975 abolished Amtrak's financial and investment advisory panel and allowed loan guarantees to be applied

---

[20] *Trains*, May 1975, p. 54.

[21] Ibid.

[22] Public Law 93–496.

to leases.[23] It also lifted a salary restriction of $60,000 per year contained in the 1972 act, substituting a limit of $85,000 per year. Congress felt that a chronically unprofitable enterprise needed a salary limit as a constraint on its expenditures, but that $60,000 per year was not competitive in the industry. The grant contained in the 1975 act was a supplemental $63 million for the current fiscal year, which brought the total overall authorization to Amtrak to $1 billion—$118 million per year. For the future, the act authorized $350 million for fiscal 1976 and $255 million for fiscal 1977 as an operating subsidy. This act initiated direct capital grants to Amtrak, apparently in the recognition that standard borrowing procedures were inappropriate to an enterprise now lacking any prospect of profitability.

The act directed Amtrak to establish on-board immigration and customs procedures for its international trains. It also adapted Amtrak's scheduling to the new federal fiscal year which starts October 1. Finally, the act extended a provision of the 1974 act that allowed the secretary of transportation to authorize grants up to 60 percent of the cost for conversion of railroad stations to intermodal terminals.

As late as 1975, Amtrak remained an operator of passenger trains as distinct from a railroad because it did not own track. In the reorganization of the bankrupt northeastern railroads into Conrail under the Regional Rail Reorganization Act of 1973[24] and the Railroad Revitalization and Regulatory Reform Act of 1976,[25] Amtrak acquired from the Penn Central its 456-mile line from Washington to Boston, plus branches of 62 miles from New Haven to Springfield, Massachusetts, and 103 miles from Philadelphia to Harrisburg—a total of 621 miles of route ranging from two to six tracks. Amtrak was obligated to pay Conrail $87 million for the trackage over the course of eight years.

In an enactment of February 5, 1976, Congress provided $1.6 billion over a five-year period for upgrading the corridor. An additional $150 million in federal money, to be matched by state funds, was provided for improvements in stations, fences along the right-of-way, and other auxiliary investments. The entire project entailed installing 420 track-miles of welded rails, replacing 900,000 ties, cleaning or replacing most of the ballast, realigning approximately fifty curves, rebuilding the tunnels through New York and Baltimore, replacing or modifying 600 bridges, modifying the existing electrification between

[23] Public Law 94–24.
[24] Public Law 93–236.
[25] Public Law 94–210.

Washington and New Haven, and extending the electrification from New Haven to Boston.

Also turned over to Amtrak in 1976 were eighty-three miles of the former Michigan Central main line from Michigan City, Indiana, to Kalamazoo, Michigan. This trackage was part of Amtrak's Chicago–Detroit and Chicago–Port Huron routes, but Conrail preferred to send freight to the former Michigan Central via a major yard which the New York Central had built at Elkhart, Indiana. Amtrak also acquired twelve miles of right-of-way near Albany, New York, on which it planned to replace track which the Penn Central had removed when passenger service was discontinued via the former New York Central main line.

The acquisition of the northeast corridor swelled Amtrak's labor costs. By the end of 1976, it employed 7,600 people on the northeast corridor, including dispatchers, towermen, and other train control personnel whose work had previously been charged to Amtrak only in its cost-plus contracts.

The development of Amtrak's statutory authority led to a great increase in the size of the system. If Amtrak were viewed as a railroad in 1975, it was the nineteenth largest in the United States in terms of revenue.[26] Acquisition of the northeast corridor line and the two minor pieces of trackage made Amtrak indisputably a railroad, approximately the ninth largest in revenue in the United States by 1977. The corporation's employment rose from 807 at the end of 1972 to 18,400 in December 1976.[27] The route structure grew from 23,606 miles in 1971 at the outset, somewhat less than half the preexisting passenger mileage, to 24,836 miles in 1976.[28] By July 1976, Amtrak had on order or in service 381 locomotives, 727 cars, and 13 turbine units, which together were expected largely to reequip the system.[29] The new equipment was to be of three types: Amfleet coaches with relatively dense seating for daytime service; bilevel equipment modeled on Santa Fe cars for transcontinental service; and conventional low-level cars for overnight trains east of Chicago. All were to be electrically heated.

Amtrak bought the Beech Grove passenger car shop of the Penn Central in Indianapolis, and by 1977 had acquired nineteen smaller facilities throughout the country for servicing its locomotives

---

[26] *Trains*, December 1975, p. 22.

[27] *Background on Amtrak* (Washington, D.C.: National Railroad Passenger Corporation, 1977), p. 19.

[28] *Trains*, April 1976, pp. 8–10.

[29] *Trains*, July 1976, p. 10.

and cars.[30] By September 30, 1976, the corporation had acquired 263 of the 495 stations its trains served.[31] By 1977 it had built new stations for Cincinnati, Jacksonville, Port Huron, Catlettsburg (Ky.), Worcester, Richmond (Va.), Roanoke, Bluefield (W.Va.), Cumberland, Cleveland, Duluth, and Parkersburg. Stations were under construction or being designed for Rochester, Richmond (Calif.), Miami, Canton, New Carrollton (Md.), and Minneapolis–St. Paul.[32] Amtrak became a member of the Association of American Railroads' Board of Directors in 1976.

Amtrak's statutory history through 1977 might, accordingly, be viewed as an unbroken series of political successes for the corporation's proponents, but the Amtrak Improvement Act of 1978[33] provided elements both favorable and hostile to those interests. This act provided a $613 million subsidy for operating expenses and $130 million for capital expenditures. A sum of $27 million was provided for converting the electrical system of the northeast corridor lines to 60-cycle AC current. Amtrak was authorized to provide commuter service by agreement with state, local, or regional transportation authorities. The statutory description of Amtrak as "a for-profit corporation" was modified to read "operated and managed as a for-profit corporation": Congress had recognized the impossibility of making the service profitable. Most important, the secretary of transportation was directed to present preliminary and final recommendations for a new Amtrak route structure based on the usual criteria, including adequacy of service by other modes. The final recommendation was required by December 31, 1978, and the system was frozen from January 1, 1978, until October 1, 1979. If either house voted a resolution of disapproval of the plan within ninety days of continuous session, the secretary was obligated to present an alternative plan within forty-five days.

Secretary of Transportation Brock Adams's plan proved to be a greatly reduced network, dropping some 12,000 miles of route, including the *Floridian*, the *Crescent* (which Amtrak acquired from the Southern Railway early in 1979), the services via the Santa Fe and former Northern Pacific main lines, and most of the purely local services, including the trains operated under section 403(b). The transcontinental services were to be reduced to three: one via the former Great Northern main line; one via Kansas City, Denver, and

---

[30] *Background on Amtrak*, p. 16.
[31] Amtrak Annual Report, 1976, pp. 12–13.
[32] Ibid.
[33] Public Law 95–421.

the Union Pacific main line, dividing at Ogden, Utah, for routes to Oakland and Los Angeles; and a third thrice weekly via the Southern Pacific between New Orleans and Los Angeles. If implemented, the plan would have reduced Amtrak's network by some 43 percent of its total mileage, which had risen to about 27,000.

Although neither house of Congress saw fit to vote disapproval of the plan within the time provided, the proposed reduction brought forth considerable congressional opposition. Pressure to preserve the *Crescent* and the *Montrealer* was particularly heavy. By way of compromise, Amtrak eliminated the *Floridian, Hilltopper* (the trans–West Virginia service via the Norfolk & Western main line), *National Limited* (New York–St. Louis), *Lone Star* (Chicago–Texas via the Santa Fe), and *North Coast Hiawatha* (the Seattle service via the former Northern Pacific main line). The cuts in the system amounted to about 16 percent of Amtrak's mileage, reducing the total operating after October 1, 1979 to 22,237.[34]

Amtrak shortly thereafter established the *Desert Wind* from Ogden, Utah, to Los Angeles, and a train subsidized by the state of Illinois from Chicago to Peoria.[35] With these additions the system amounted to 23,515 miles at the end of 1975, a net reduction of about 13 percent.

Simultaneously with the reduction, Congress enacted the Amtrak Reorganization Act of 1979,[36] which in the short run would make further discontinuances more difficult. Specifically, the law provided that a long-distance train be retained if the anticipated avoidable loss per passenger-mile for fiscal 1980 is not over seven cents and the ridership is not less than 150 passenger-miles per train-mile. For short-distance trains the criteria were nine cents per passenger-mile and 80 passenger-miles per train mile. The act set goals of a 50 percent improvement in on-time performance within three years, plus the implementation of a system-wide average speed of 55 miles per hour. Similarly, Amtrak was required to cover 44 percent of operating expenses by fares by the end of fiscal 1982 and 50 percent by 1985; the corporation was required to report to Congress on allocation of costs by route by April 30, 1980.

By January 1, 1981, Amtrak must provide Congress and the president with a plan to include "a zero-based assessment of all operating practices and implementation of changes to achieve the minimum use of employees consistent with safe operations and adequate service,"

[34] *Traffic World*, September 3, 1979, p. 11.
[35] *Trains*, January 1980, p. 8.
[36] Public Law 96–73, September 29, 1979.

a systematic plan for optimizing the ratio of train size to passenger demand; a program for time reduction on all trains in the basic system; a training program to ensure on-time departures and priorities of passenger trains over freight trains; and a program to reduce losses on food and beverage service. It must also establish a cooperative marketing campaign with the Department of Energy, the Federal Highway Administration, and the Environmental Protection Agency. Technical Assistance panels are authorized to participate with the states in establishing section 403(b) services on the grounds that "state participation in subsidizing interstate rail passenger service has, for the most part, been unworkable." The act exempts the corporation from "buy-American" requirements when new cars cannot be bought domestically in a reasonable time.

It provides operating grants to Amtrak of $630.9 million in fiscal 1980 and $675 million in 1981, and it provides capital grants of $203 million in fiscal 1980, $244 million in 1981, and $254 million in 1982. The capital grants are expected to be used mainly for reequipping the eastern overnight services with single-level cars and supplying track changes for rerouting the *Broadway Limited* and *San Francisco Zephyr*.

In sum, the act of 1979 furnished Amtrak with a security of financial expectations that previous enactments lacked, but it imposed a set of rules on the corporation that will be increasingly difficult to satisfy. As Amtrak's operating experience demonstrates, the act's requirements concerning speed, punctuality, and the relation of revenue to cost will be difficult or impossible to meet.

3

Amtrak's Operating Experience

Given the institutional arrangements that Congress provided for Amtrak, there was no a priori reason why rail passenger volume should decline further. The remaining demand had been consolidated on fewer than half the preexisting trains, and federal subsidies would inevitably affect people's choices of transportation modes at the margin. In fact, the establishment of Amtrak produced a high degree of stability in railroad ridership. From 1972 to 1977, as table 2 indicates, Amtrak did experience increases of 12.5 percent in the number of passengers and 29.9 percent in passenger-miles, but the increases resulted largely from expansion of the system to include more trains. Route-miles increased 11.5 percent and train-miles 21.2 percent over the same period.

The petroleum shortage of November 1973–April 1974 led to a temporary sharp increase in output throughout the Amtrak system. Passenger trips rose from 7.47 million in the same period a year earlier to 8.87 million, but fell back to 7.73 million a year afterward. Similarly, passenger-miles in the three periods began at 1.52 billion, rose to 2.21 billion, and then fell to 1.76 billion.[1] Rail service continued to fail at retaining the passengers it attracted in emergencies. The Baltimore & Ohio Railroad's *Capitol Limited* doubled its first-class ridership during an airline strike in 1966, but the secular trend against it resumed immediately.[2] In this instance, the secular trend was mildly positive.

Amtrak reports its operations under three headings: northeast corridor (Boston–New York–Washington with branches, Philadelphia–

---

[1] *A Reexamination of the Amtrak Route Structure* (Washington. D.C.: Department of Transportation, May 1978), p. 2–10.

[2] *Trains*, November 1966, p. 6.

TABLE 2
AMTRAK OUTPUT, 1972–1978

Year	Ridership (millions)	Passenger-Miles (millions)	Route-Miles (thousands)	Train-Miles (millions)
1972	16.6	3,038	23	26
1973	16.9	3,806	22	27
1974	18.8	4,258	24	29
1975	17.4	3,939	26	30
1976	18.6	4,221	26	31
1977	19.2	4,333	26	33
1978	18.9	4,169	26	32
Percentage increase	13.8	37.2	13.0	18.8

SOURCES: National Railroad Passenger Corporation, *Background on Amtrak* (1977), p. 27; Amtrak Annual Report, 1977, p. 24; Amtrak Performance Measure Reports, 1978–1979.

Harrisburg, and New Haven–Springfield), short-haul (up to 500 miles), and long-haul (mainly services requiring overnight travel). The system's 1972–1976 gain in ridership was mainly on short-distance routes outside the northeast corridor (see table 3). The

TABLE 3
AMTRAK RIDERSHIP, 1972–1978

Fiscal Year	Northeast Corridor Number (thousands)	Percent	Short Haul Number (thousands)	Percent	Long Haul Number (thousands)	Percent
1972	8,150	59	1,389	10	4,200	31
1973	8,697	59	1,469	10	4,560	31
1974	9,974	60	2,538	15	4,139	25
1975	9,596	61	2,527	16	3,709	23
1976	9,865	59	2,914	17	4,089	24
1977	10,939	57	3,356	17	4,909	26
1978	10,348	55	3,378	18	5,147	27

SOURCES: "Four Years of Amtrak Operation," updated, unpublished DOT study; U.S. Congress, House of Representatives, *Department of Transportation and Related Agencies Appropriations for 1979*, Hearings before a Subcommittee of the Committee on Appropriations, 95th Congress, 2nd session (1978) (hereafter cited as House Appropriations Hearing, 1979), pp. 882–883; Amtrak Public Affairs Office, unpublished data.

corridor services accounted fairly consistently for about 60 percent of Amtrak riders and thus approximated the system's overall rate of increase from 1972 to 1976. The long-haul services, after a peak in fiscal 1973, lost ridership overall, falling from a 31 percent share of the total in 1973 to only 24 percent in 1976. Such increase in ridership as Amtrak had resulted largely from the establishment of services under subsidy under section 403(b), experimental trains added under Amtrak's own funding, and an increase in frequency on the midwestern corridor services. The acquisition of the northeast corridor trackage in 1976 swelled Amtrak's ridership with the commuters previously included in Penn Central figures.

The nature of the ridership increase also emerges from the breakdown of passengers by first-class and coach in table 4. First-class ridership was relatively stable with a marked peak in 1974; the increase was almost entirely in coach. With the acquisition of the northeast corridor, Amtrak began to carry substantial numbers of passengers on multiple-ride tickets, without leaving record of their class of travel. These have been reported as "unknown," though virtually all are probably coach. Thus the relative decline of Amtrak's first-class passengers is probably an accurate reflection of its trend in ridership composition.

It should be noted that the length of the run by which Amtrak classifies trains does not necessarily indicate the length of the trip.

TABLE 4

AMTRAK RIDERSHIP BY CLASS OF SERVICE, 1973–1978 [a]

	First-Class		Coach		Unknown	
Fiscal Year	Number (thousands)	Percent	Number (thousands)	Percent	Number (thousands)	Percent
1973	744	5.6	12,615	94.4	—	—
1974	822	4.8	16,307	95.2	—	—
1975	702	4.4	15,414	95.6	—	—
1976	743	4.1	15,633	87.0	1,597	8.9
1977	699	3.7	15,097	79.9	3,093	16.4
1978	675	3.6	15,696	82.7	2,603	13.7

[a] Prior to 1973, railroads did not report first-class versus coach ridership systematically to Amtrak.
SOURCE: U.S. Department of Transportation, Federal Railroad Administration, Office of Rail Systems Analysis and Information, Information and Statistics Division, *Amtrak Origin and Destination by Route*, 1973–1978.

TABLE 5
AMTRAK RIDERSHIP BY CLASS OF SERVICE,
CHICAGO–LOS ANGELES, CHICAGO–NEW YORK, 1973–1978

	Chicago–Los Angeles			Chicago–New York		
Fiscal Year	First-Class	Coach	Total	First-Class	Coach	Total
1973	57,854	240,311	298,165	22,841	170,235	193,876
1974	62,421	263,184	325,605	41,010	202,131	243,141
1975	48,211	224,709	272,920	52,058	153,661	206,719
1976	43,114	263,344	306,760[a]	37,694	145,643	183,758[a]
1977	34,520	252,764	287,862[a]	30,514	133,350	164,861[a]
1978	32,783	232,458	266,161[a]	22,857	104,069	127,979[a]

[a] Includes "unknown" category.
SOURCE: U.S. Department of Transportation, Federal Railroad Administration, Office of Rail Systems Analysis and Information, Information and Statistics Division, *Amtrak Origin and Destination by Route,* 1973–1978.

Amtrak's average length of trip is about 270 miles,[3] with relatively few passengers riding the longer distances. Only 3 percent of passengers on the Los Angeles–Seattle train ride the full distance, and on the Chicago–Los Angeles train, which enjoys the greatest long-distance ridership, the number of end-to-end passengers rises to 15 percent only in summer months.[4]

Ridership of Amtrak's principal trains from Chicago to the East and West coasts, the services to New York and Los Angeles respectively, appears in table 5. Both services show a decline in utilization after the 1974 peak, and in both, first-class ridership declined more rapidly than coach for most years. This continued the pattern of relative shares that characterized the pre-Amtrak experience.

Corroborating evidence of a decline in ridership is found in the data on passenger-miles per train-mile—that is, the average number of passengers on a train at any one time—gathered annually by the Interstate Commerce Commission. For the period October 1974–February 1975, Amtrak produced 126.8 passenger-miles per train-mile, but the figure declined to 103.8 in fiscal 1976 and to 96.6 in fiscal

[3] U.S. Congress, House of Representatives, *Department of Transportation and Related Agencies Appropriations for 1979,* Hearings before a Subcommittee of the Committee on Appropriations, 95th Congress, 2nd session (1978) (hereafter cited as House Appropriations Hearing, 1979), p. 927.
[4] Ibid., p. 926.

TABLE 6

AMTRAK PROJECTIONS OF 1979 RIDERSHIP, 1974–1977

Year of Projection	Ridership Projected for 1979 (millions)
1974	37.0
1975	29.2
1976	20.6
1977	21.3
1978[a]	20.3
1979[a]	19.6

[a] Fiscal year (October 1–September 30).
SOURCES: "An Analysis of Amtrak's Five Year Plan," General Accounting Office, Report no. PAD–78–51 (1978); Amtrak Performance Measure Report, November 1978; April 1979.

1977.[5] In part, the change reflects the expansion of the system, because the various experimental routes and state-supported services have lower riderships than the basic network.

Because of such distortions, the unadjusted time series of Amtrak's absolute number of riders shown in table 2, which suggests an increase in utilization of the system, is undoubtedly misleading. In fact, Amtrak has revised downward its projections for future ridership in each succeeding annual five-year plan presented to Congress, as indicated in table 6.

Demand Conditions

Amtrak's experience to date has occasioned a small and still incomplete, but generally consistent, literature on the demand for its services. All agree on a basic point: Amtrak is confronted by relatively high elasticities of demand with respect to price. In eastern markets, the corporation reports a price elasticity of demand for regular one-way fares of −0.67, the lowest in the system. Such trips are mostly business-related and, to a greater extent than elsewhere on Amtrak, air-competitive. In contrast, Amtrak reports that promotional fares in the same geographic area have an elasticity of −1.45.[6]

[5] "Amtrak's Subsidy Needs Cannot Be Reduced without Reducing Service," General Accounting Office, Report no. CED–78–86 (1978), p. 49.
[6] "Amtrak Fare Elasticity Model," Amtrak internal memorandum, p. II–14. Data are for fiscal 1977.

In other areas, where Amtrak's ridership is more discretionary or recreational, elasticities are greater. Amtrak calculates an overall elasticity of demand with respect to price for one-way fares—all regions, all markets—of about -2.2.[7] These high price elasticities reflect the abundance of alternative modes in all markets. Amtrak has consistently found relatively high cross-elasticities of demand with other carriers, measured as the percentage change in ridership of either mode consequent upon a 1 percent change in fare of the other. In northeast corridor markets, the cross-elasticity between rail and air is 0.6,[8] and that between rail and bus is 1.29.[9] This implies that even in the area where Amtrak is most time-competitive with planes, the service is mainly a rival to buses.

Unfortunately, Amtrak has produced no statistically significant estimates of the income elasticity of demand for its services, owing to problems of adequacy of data. The corporation takes the high incidence of discretionary or recreational travel to mean that the income elasticity is now positive.[10] The evidence that Amtrak's ridership is highly discretionary is unambiguous. Travel is least discretionary in the northeast corridor, most so on the transcontinental trains. Northeast corridor trains are divided into the Metroliners, fast, multiple-unit trains operating at a premium fare, and conventional trains of Amfleet equipment hauled by locomotives. As would be expected, business travel is highly concentrated on the Metroliners, Amtrak's most air-competitive service. Amtrak has sampled passengers with respect to purpose of their trips, as shown in table 7.

A private survey of passengers on Amtrak's major western transcontinental trains also found most rail travel to be discretionary. Professor Richard L. Day of the University of Idaho supervised a survey of passengers on Amtrak's services between Chicago and Seattle and Los Angeles, with findings as summarized in table 8. The high percentage of discretionary travel is also evident in the high percentage of trips that would not have occurred except by train, as shown in table 9. Many such riders are former railroad pass holders, since Amtrak honors their passes. About 4.4 percent of Amtrak's passengers ride on passes, but these are highly concentrated on the long-distance services. About 8.1 percent of long-haul pas-

---

[7] Ibid., p. II–8.

[8] Ibid., p. II–12.

[9] Ibid., p. II–13. An econometric model of 1976 by A. T. Kearney found a virtually zero cross-elasticity between rail and bus, however. *The Bus Industry*, ICC Bureau of Economics (May 1978), p. 113.

[10] Letter to the author of Robert E. Gall, director of marketing research of Amtrak, July 20, 1978.

TABLE 7

AMTRAK RIDERSHIP BY PURPOSE OF TRIP, CA. 1976

(percent)

| | Northeast Corridor | | Outside Northeast Corridor |
Purpose	Metroliner	Amfleet	
Business	64	37	9
Personal affairs	22	39	26
School	0	6	4
Vacation	14	16	62

SOURCE: U.S. Congress, House of Representatives, *Department of Transportation and Related Agencies Appropriations for 1978*, Hearings before a Subcommittee of the Committee on Appropriation, 95th Congress, 1st session (1977), p. 564.

TABLE 8

AMTRAK RIDERSHIP BY PURPOSE OF TRIP, APRIL–JUNE 1978, CHICAGO–LOS ANGELES AND CHICAGO–SEATTLE SERVICES

Purpose	Percent
Business or work	9
Recreation or vacation	27
Visit to friends or relatives	50
Personal affairs	10
School	4

SOURCE: "Summary of Findings, Day and Associates' Passenger Train Surveys," Spring 1978, from Richard L. Day, Department of Geography, University of Idaho, Moscow, Idaho.

sengers ride on passes, as compared with 2.5 percent in the northeast corridor. Specifically, 15.8 percent of Chicago–Los Angeles passengers and approximately 13.2 percent on the two Chicago–Seattle trains ride on passes.[11]

The high percentage of discretionary travel also manifests itself in the low percentage of passengers who would otherwise opt for bus. The figures in table 9 are probably biased by the availability of rival trains between the Twin Cities and Seattle on parallel routes of the Burlington Northern and the absence of competing bus service along

[11] *Report to the President and the Congress on the Effectiveness of the Rail Passenger Service Act of 1970*, Interstate Commerce Commission, March 15, 1978, p. 80.

TABLE 9

Mode	Percent
Automobile	22
Plane	34
Bus	12
Another train	7
Hitchhike	0
Would not have made trip	24

Source: "Summary of Findings, Day and Associates' Passenger Train Surveys," Spring 1978, from Richard L. Day, Department of Geography, University of Idaho, Moscow, Idaho.

much of the former Great Northern route. Consequently, the number of passengers who would choose an alternative train is presumably higher and the number who would alternatively choose a bus is lower than for Amtrak as a whole. For a more general sample of Amtrak, approximately 23 percent of passengers reported that they would, in absence of the trains, take buses.[12]

Superficially, it is surprising that Amtrak's percentage of passengers who would otherwise take buses is so low, considering that the demographic characteristics of Amtrak and Greyhound passengers are quite similar (see table 10). The reason that Amtrak has failed to attract many bus-competitive passengers is probably its lesser frequency in all areas except the northeast corridor. Amtrak produced a route forecasting model (table 11), based on seventy-one observations of changes on thirty-nine routes between 1974 and 1976, in which it found the highest sensitivity among the variables for schedule frequency. By econometric standards, the model is an odd one in not including fares as a variable, especially in application to an enterprise with mainly elastic demands. The implication of the model that schedule frequency is the most significant variable in Amtrak's ridership is consistent with several observed events in Amtrak's history. Notably, Amtrak's inception, coinciding with annihilation of about half the existing passenger trains, did not significantly alter the

[12] "A Survey of American Attitudes toward Transportation," prepared for the Department of Transportation by Peter D. Hart Research Associates (Department of Transportation, Report no. DOT-1-78-1, January 1978), p. 52. In this survey 48 percent responded they would otherwise use automobiles and 22 percent, planes. The remaining 7 percent were unreported.

secular decline of bus ridership in 1971. Similarly, the great shortfall of Amtrak's passenger volumes relative to the expectations of its original proponents is consistent with passengers' on the margin between Amtrak and bus lines being highly influenced by schedule

TABLE 10

DEMOGRAPHIC CHARACTERISTICS OF GREYHOUND
AND AMTRAK PASSENGERS
(percent)

	Bus	Train
Sex		
Male	39.0	40.5
Female	52.0	59.5
Not reported	9.0	—
Education		
Grade school or less	9.0	4.6
High school or less	35.0	38.6
Age		
Under 18	5.0	6.7
18–24	27.0	21.0
25–34	17.0	20.8
35–44	9.0	12.7
45–54	12.0	12.0
55 and over	28.0	26.7
Not reported	3.0	—
Household Income		
Under $5,000	18.0	15.6
$5,000–14,999	47.0	36.1
$15,000 and over	20.0	40.2
Not reported	15.0	—
Purpose of Trip		
Business or work	11.0	8.8
To and from school	4.0	3.5
Vacation, recreation, etc.	77.0	61.6
Personal affairs	7.0	16.9
Other	12.0[a]	9.1

[a] Does not add to 100. Some respondents made multiple responses.

SOURCES: Amtrak Passenger Assessment Survey, June 1976; Greyhound On-Board Passenger Survey, August 1976, submitted by the Greyhound Corporation to the House Committee on Interstate and Foreign Commerce, April 3, 1978, with cover letter of John E. Adkins, group vice-president for transportation to Congressman Joe Skubitz.

TABLE 11
Amtrak's Route Forecasting Model

Sample contains 71 observations of annual changes on 39 routes served by Amtrak. Sample covered changes between 1974 and 1975 and between 1975 and 1976 on routes with service in both years.

FORMULA

$R\% = -0.38 + 1.109\,F\% + 0.319\,E + 0.073\,T\% + 4.964\,P\% -18.325\,ED$

S.E.	(0.022)	(0.07)	(0.041)	(2.37)	(3.198)
t	(51.265)	(4.577)	(1.797)	(2.095)	(−5.73)
Significance level	(99.9%)	(99.9%)	(95%)	(97.5%)	(99.9%)

R squared = 0.978,   F = 557.8,   S.E. of estimate = 12.264

Where $R\%$ = percentage change of ridership on any route in a year

$F\%$ = percentage change of frequency on any route in a year where frequency is expressed as train-mile-days/(route miles times 365 days)

E = absolute change in the percentage of train days having new equipment (Amfleet and Turboliner)

$T\%$ = percentage change of Amtrak on-time performance on any route in a year

$P\%$ = percentage change of population in states along the routes

ED = 1 for recovery from energy shortage (1974–1975)
0 for no shortage in either year (1975–1976)

NOTE: Energy shortage is defined as two months where 50% of households report difficulty obtaining gas.

INTERPRETATION

Standard error of coefficients (S.E.)
There is a 68% probability that the coefficients will fall in a range of plus or minus one standard error. For example, the coefficient of Amtrak frequency will fall in a range of 1.109 = 0.022.

t statistics
This statistic gives the significant level which is the probability that the estimated coefficient is statistically significantly different from zero.

R squared
97.8% of the variation in ridership percentage change has been explained by the model.

Standard error of estimate
There is a 68% probability that actual ridership percentage change will fall

(Table continues on next page)

TABLE 11 (continued)

in a range of ±12.264 percentage points of the percent change estimated by the above formula.

F-ratio

There is a 99.9% probability that the ridership is related to the explanatory variables stated on the right-hand side of the above formula.

SOURCE: House Appropriations Hearing, 1979, pp. 956–957.

frequency. As the consideration of costs in the next section indicates, increasing Amtrak's frequency to levels approximating those of Greyhound and Trailways would be extremely costly.

Interestingly, there is nothing in the model to imply any high degree of responsiveness of passenger volume to the quality of service, in the usual sense of on-board luxury, even though the establishment of the system was based on a presumption of a high demand elasticity with respect to this factor. First-class ridership has continued to decline relative to coach, and Amtrak has responded much as the railroads did. It dropped Pullman cars on the *Inter-American, Cardinal,* and *Panama Limited* in 1978, although it subsequently restored them on the latter two in the face of ICC pressure.[13] Amtrak also modified on-train food services: "The introduction of Amfleet and Turboliners has changed On-Board Service procedures. Modern preparation methods are employed and include automatic beverage dispensers, prepared food items and containerized delivery systems allowing us to provide more variety to our passengers while reducing waste and loss."[14] Such actions drew the same response the railroads' actions had drawn: in 1973 Anthony Haswell accused Amtrak of trying to get rid of the *Floridian,* the weakest train in its basic network, by downgrading the quality of service.[15]

Fare Policy

In view of the demand conditions, Amtrak presumably pursued a conscious fare policy in some effort to optimize. Such efforts were surprisingly free of constraints, for Amtrak was subject to ICC regulation only of the quality of its service, not its fares. In addition,

---

[13] *Trains,* March 1978, p. 13.

[14] Amtrak's Submission, House Appropriations Hearing, 1979, p. 977.

[15] U.S. Congress, Senate, *Amtrak Oversight and Authorization,* Hearings on S. 1763 before the Surface Transportation Subcommittee of Committee on Commerce, 93rd Congress, 1st session (1973), p. 40.

Amtrak was not subject to normal cost constraints, being operated under heavy subsidy granted by an apparently willing Congress. This set of institutional arrangements can probably not be defended; recommendations for deregulation of intercity passenger fares have typically exempted subsidized local-service airlines on the ground that there was no presumption of optimality in consequent resource allocation under the circumstances.[16]

Amtrak inherited the fare structure of previous railroad passenger services. As might be expected in a chronically unprofitable, rapidly declining activity, there was little consistency in the regulated fares. In general, coach fares were intermediate between air coach and bus, but higher in the northeastern United States than elsewhere. Amtrak, relieved almost entirely of the constraints of making interline rates with other carriers, did simplify and rationalize the fare structure to some extent. It replaced interline fares with single, equalized fares in opposite directions, lowered the age for children's fares from five to two, and ended discounts for ordinary round-trip journeys. It also standardized rules for family-plan round trips, which had varied widely by railroad. Similarly, Amtrak made selective increases and decreases in ordinary fares by route to produce greater geographic consistency. Fares continue to differ by route, however. Amtrak coach fares vary from five to ten cents per mile, and first-class fares in roomettes from eight to seventeen cents.[17]

Given Amtrak's rivalry with air and highway carriers, the overall rate of fare increases in response to inflation is the most important and most controversial of its fare policies. In general, Amtrak's first-class fares have approximated air coach fares, and its coach fares have risen at about the same rate as the transportation component of the Consumer Price Index, or 6 percent per year. However, this is only about two-thirds the overall rate of inflation.[18] In consequence, the spread between rail coach and bus fares has narrowed, and this is alleged to be the principal source of damage caused by Amtrak to rival carriers (see chapter 4).

Cost Conditions

Amtrak's costs have been studied in great detail, partly for the corporation's own purposes and partly because of continual concern

---

[16] See, for example, George W. Hilton et al., "The National Transportation Policy: Report of a Task Force to the President of the United States" (1964).

[17] *Reexamination of Amtrak Route Structure*, pp. 7–2, 7–3.

[18] House Appropriations Hearing, 1979, p. 909.

TABLE 12
AMTRAK REVENUE AND COST PER REVENUE PASSENGER-MILE, FISCAL 1977

Route	Revenue per Revenue Passenger-Mile (cents)	Cost per Revenue Passenger-Mile (cents)	Profit (Loss) per Revenue Passenger-Mile (cents)
Northeast Corridor			
New York City–Washington (Metroliner)	13.1	19.3	(6.2)
New York City–Washington (Conventional)	12.1	28.0	(15.9)
New Haven–Springfield	6.9	44.5	(37.6)
New York City–Harrisburg	6.5	23.1	(16.6)
Northeast corridor total	10.9	22.9	(12.0)
Short Haul			
Chicago–Carbondale	9.0	20.7	(11.7)
Chicago–Detroit	7.9	23.8	(15.9)
Chicago–Dubuque	16.5	26.7	(10.2)
Chicago–Milwaukee	7.1	44.1	(37.0)
Chicago–Port Huron	11.9	39.7	(27.8)
Chicago–Quincy	12.2	18.8	(6.6)
Chicago–St. Louis	8.7	19.9	(11.2)
Los Angeles–San Diego	8.8	20.6	(11.8)
Minneapolis–Duluth	10.4	18.6	(8.2)
New York City–Buffalo–Detroit	8.1	24.0	(15.9)
New York City–Montreal	11.2	26.8	(15.6)
Oakland–Bakersfield	5.9	27.4	(21.5)
Seattle–Portland	4.9	22.1	(17.2)
Seattle–Vancouver	6.6	21.8	(15.2)
Washington–Cincinnati	6.8	18.7	(11.9)
Washington–Martinsburg	4.8	36.0	(31.2)
Short haul total	8.5	24.5	(16.0)
Long Haul			
Boston–Newport News	3.0	5.4	(2.4)
Chicago–Florida	7.4	28.0	(20.6)
Chicago–Houston	7.3	24.8	(17.5)
Chicago–Laredo	7.1	34.8	(27.7)
Chicago–Los Angeles	9.1	21.8	(12.7)
Chicago–New Orleans	6.4	14.5	(8.1)
Chicago–New York City–Boston	7.6	22.6	(15.0)

TABLE 12 (continued)

Route	Revenue per Revenue Passenger-Mile (cents)	Cost per Revenue Passenger-Mile (cents)	Profit (Loss) Revenue per Passenger-Mile (cents)
Chicago–New York City– Washington	9.0	26.5	(17.0)
Chicago–San Francisco	9.4	28.9	(19.5)
Chicago–Seattle (North)	8.6	29.9	(21.3)
Chicago–Seattle (South)	8.2	34.2	(26.0)
Chicago–Washington	6.1	29.0	(22.9)
Kansas City–New York City– Washington	9.1	31.0	(22.0)
Los Angeles–New Orleans	8.1	22.9	(14.8)
Los Angeles–Seattle	7.2	18.7	(11.5)
New York–Florida	6.9	18.8	(11.9)
New York–Savannah	7.5	15.8	(8.3)
Seattle–Salt Lake City	6.7	15.0	(8.3)
Washington–Montreal	8.4	29.7	(21.3)
Long haul total	7.4	21.7	(14.3)
Total (excluding northeast corridor)	7.5	22.2	(14.7)
Northeast Corridor Total	10.9	22.9	(12.0)
System Total	8.3	22.3	(14.0)

SOURCE: Interstate Commerce Commission, *Report to the President and the Congress on the Effectiveness of the Rail Passenger Service Act of 1970*, March 15, 1978, pp. 71–72.

by the House Appropriations Subcommittee and various executive bodies. Amtrak's cost reporting has received general approval from its own auditors and the General Accounting Office.[19]

In fiscal 1977 Amtrak's average total cost of moving passengers was 22.3 cents per passenger-mile. This was quite consistent over the types of service: 22.9 cents in the northeast corridor, 24.5 cents in short-haul services, and 21.7 cents in long-haul services. (The figures are somewhat biased by the inclusion of Boston–Newport News as a long-haul route, even though most of the passenger-miles are accounted for by Boston–New York trains.) With an average fare of 8.3 cents per mile, Amtrak loses 14.0 cents per passenger-mile. Again, the experience is consistent among services. Trains in the northeast

---

[19] See, for example, "Amtrak's Subsidy Needs Cannot Be Reduced without Reducing Service" and Amtrak Annual Report, 1976, p. 31.

corridor lose 12.0 cents per passenger-mile; short-haul services, 16.0 cents per passenger-mile; and long-haul, 14.3 cents. No route is profitable, but the Metroliners of the northeast corridor service, with a loss of 6.2 cents per passenger-mile, are the least unprofitable. The most unprofitable services are both short hauls—New Haven–Springfield and Chicago–Milwaukee—each with costs exceeding 44 cents per passenger-mile and net losses of over 37 cents per passenger-mile.

Operating results by route, including loss per passenger, are shown in table 13. Amtrak lost $24.14 per passenger overall: $6.45 on the Metroliners, $8.94 on other northeast corridor trains, $15.70 on short-haul services, and $64.77 on long-haul services. The highest absolute loss was $122.55 per passenger on New York–Florida trains, a relatively heavily utilized service.

Figures on a train-mile basis are similar. For the entire system, Amtrak's cost was $21.56 per train-mile in fiscal 1977 compared with revenue of $8.06, a net loss of $13.50. By this measure, owing to their larger absolute number of passengers, the northeast corridor trains are the most unprofitable, losing $15.57 per train-mile, versus $12.48 for short-haul trains elsewhere and $13.18 for long-haul services.[20]

Amtrak's cost trend has been strongly upward. Operating expenses rose from $309 million in 1972 to $681 million in 1976, an increase of 121 percent. In contrast, the cost of all railroad freight operations increased only 42 percent. Similarly, Amtrak's operating expense per car-mile rose from $1.46 in 1972 to $2.76 in 1976, an increase of 89 percent, whereas railroad operating expense per freight car-mile increased only 49 percent in the same period.[21]

Comparison with the Southern Railway is especially instructive. The Southern's average total cost per passenger-mile rose from 18.2 cents in 1972 to 26.4 cents in 1976, about 45 percent, which is slightly more than the percentage cost increase for railroad freight operations overall. The Southern's cost per passenger-mile in 1977 was 26.6 cents, compared with Amtrak's 22.3 cents.[22] The Southern over this period dropped its secondary trains and was operating only its *Southern Crescent*, a labor-intensive overnight train with Pullman, dining, and lounge cars. This train is similar to Amtrak's long-distance trains, which account for about 20 percent of Amtrak's ridership but 68 percent of its losses. The Southern had the benefit of the consolidation of all its major passenger service facilities at Atlanta and

---

[20] Interstate Commerce Commission, *Report on Effectiveness*, pp. 72–73.

[21] *Reexamination of Amtrak Route Structure*, p. 2–8.

[22] Southern Consolidated System, "Expenses per Revenue Passenger-Mile," memorandum furnished to author, July 26, 1978.

TABLE 13
AMTRAK OPERATING RESULTS BY ROUTE, FISCAL 1977

Route	Revenues (thousands of dollars)	Expenses (thousands of dollars)	Operating Loss (thousands of dollars)	Percent of Total Loss	Passengers (thousands)	Loss per Passenger
Northeast Corridor						
Metroliners	36,861	49,768	12,907	—	2,000	6.45
Other routes	54,873	134,814	79,941	—	8,939	8.94
Subtotal	91,734	184,582	92,848	20.0		
Short Haul						
Chicago–Carbondale	1,893	3,887	1,994	—	143	13.94
Chicago–Detroit	4,335	11,283	6,948	—	425	16.35
Chicago–Dubuque	801	1,320	519	—	39	13.31
Chicago–Milwaukee	1,431	7,341	5,910	—	270	21.89
Chicago–Port Huron	1,981	4,924	2,943	—	93	31.65
Chicago–Quincy	1,650	2,532	882	—	86	10.26
Chicago–St. Louis	2,713	5,218	2,505	—	182	13.76
Los Angeles–San Diego	4,441	8,709	4,268	—	689	6.19
Minneapolis–Duluth	959	1,446	487	—	79	6.16
NYC–Buffalo–Detroit	8,645	22,028	13,383	—	602	22.23
New York–Montreal	2,575	5,327	2,752	—	121	22.74
Oakland–Bakersfield	694	3,109	2,415	—	91	26.54
Seattle–Portland	1,018	3,752	2,734	—	141	19.39

(Table continues on next page)

TABLE 13 (continued)

Route	Revenues (thousands of dollars)	Expenses (thousands of dollars)	Operating Loss (thousands of dollars)	Percent of Total Loss	Passengers (thousands)	Loss per Passenger
Seattle–Vancouver	583	1,808	1,225	—	88	13.91
Washington–Cincinnati	620	3,173	2,553	—	265[a]	14.06
Washington–Martinsburg	317	1,489	1,172	—	—	—
Special trains	837	837	0	—	42	—
Subtotal	35,493	88,183	52,690	11.4	3,356	15.70
Long Haul						
Boston–Newport News	5,915	9,152	3,237	—	266	12.17
Chicago–Florida	5,795	21,671	15,876	—	147	108.00
Chicago–Houston	6,976	22,079	15,103	—	263	57.43
Chicago–Laredo	2,902	13,167	10,265	—	145	70.79
Chicago–Los Angeles	19,367	43,312	23,945	—	301	79.55
Chicago–New Orleans	5,208	11,544	6,336	—	192	33.00
Chicago–NYC–Boston	7,412	20,774	13,362	—	289	46.24
Chicago–NYC–Washington	10,195	25,597	15,402	—	244	63.12
Chicago–San Francisco	14,041	41,424	27,383	—	267	102.56
Chicago–Seattle (North)	12,234	39,525	27,291	—	297	91.89
Chicago–Seattle (South)	6,236	22,149	15,913	—	205	77.62
Chicago–Washington	3,286	13,743	10,457	—	183	57.14
Kansas City–NYC–Washington	6,298	21,782	15,484	—	192	80.65
Los Angeles–New Orleans	5,708	15,579	9,861	—	107	92.16

Los Angeles–Seattle	13,065	33,024	19,959	—	474	42.11
New York–Florida	36,464	103,010	66,546	—	543	122.55
New York–Savannah	5,840	13,762	7,922	—	387	20.47
Seattle–Salt Lake	1,311	2,792	1,481	—	57	25.98
Washington–Montreal	5,298	17,444	12,146	—	350	34.70
Subtotal	173,551	491,520	317,969	68.6	4,909	64.77
Operating Total	300,778	764,285	463,507	100.0	19,204	24.14
Other Revenue	5,908	—	5,908	—	—	—
Subtotal	306,686	764,285	457,599			
Corporate Expenses		57,400	57,400			
Grand Total	306,686	821,685	514,999	—	—	—

[a] Includes Washington–Martinsburg route.

SOURCE: House Appropriations Hearing, 1979, pp. 882–883.

their integration with more general railroad locomotive and car shops. It also had the advantage of a relatively small office staff exclusively concerned with passengers, but the disadvantage of operating old diesel passenger units with high maintenance expenses.

By way of further contrast, the bus industry in 1976 carried its passengers for 4.91 cents per passenger-mile and the airlines theirs for about 7.9 cents.[23] Thus the cost inferiority of Amtrak or the Southern Railway to bus was well over 4 to 1.

The reason for Amtrak's cost inferiority to its rivals is the same problem that railroads have always had: trains are extremely labor-intensive. Congress did not, as a quid pro quo for establishing Amtrak, exact any relaxation of traditional work rules from the railroad brotherhoods. Paul Reistrup, president of Amtrak, testified in 1978 that about 85 percent of the corporation's employees were covered by union contracts and that about 65 percent of Amtrak's costs were for labor.[24] Anthony Haswell in 1972 reported the labor costs per one-way trip between Chicago and Milwaukee as $93.72 by train, $31.67 by plane, and $15.61 by bus.[25]

The most intensive study of Amtrak's cost was done by the General Accounting Office in 1978 as one of its annual audits of Amtrak's performance, required by the act of 1970. The GAO chose a single train, Amtrak 355, which departed Detroit at 5:35 P.M. and arrived in Chicago at 10:15 P.M. The train's schedule was that of the New York Central's *Twilight Limited*, the principal Chicago–Detroit train of the private railroad era. Thus, the choice of train was biased, if at all, in Amtrak's favor. Amtrak allocated expenses of $143,898 to the train for the month of June 1977 in an accounting process which the GAO considered generally correct. This sum averaged out to a cost of about $30 per passenger for a yield from fare and food service of about $12.

The costs of train 355 for the month are shown in table 14. The train operated with Conrail engine crews subject to the usual definition of 100 miles as a full day's work. The trip of 279 miles involved two districts: Detroit to Jackson, 74 miles covered in 80 minutes, and Jackson to Chicago, 205 miles traversed in 260 minutes. Accordingly, the four employees occupied in engine service ran up approximately 5.6 days' pay collectively. Engineers were receiving about $30,500 per year in 1976 and firemen $27,500, including benefits. The em-

---

[23] *Report from the American Bus Association* (Washington, D.C.: American Bus Association, 1977), p. 9.
[24] House Appropriations Hearing, 1979, p. 937.
[25] *Trains*, January 1972, p. 8.

TABLE 14
Costs of Operating Amtrak Train 355, June 1977

Item		Dollar Cost
Direct labor		
Engine crew	10,693	
Train crew	10,906	
Service crew	5,199	
Subtotal		26,798
Maintenance of equipment		20,381
Maintenance of way		16,296
Station costs		9,355
Yard operations		6,620
Sales and marketing		5,937
Depreciation, taxes, insurance		5,908
Fuel		5,849
Reservation system		5,036
Total		102,180

Source: "Should Amtrak Develop High-Speed Corridor Service outside the Northeast?" General Accounting Office, Report no. CED–78–67 (1978), p. 20.

ployees also received full reimbursement for lodging and food expenses at turnaround points.[26] In contrast, a bus driver would drive the entire route in six hours for a single day's pay. Class I bus drivers in the same year averaged about $15,490 per year.[27]

The train crew of conductor and brakemen, also Conrail employees, ran through from Detroit to Chicago, each receiving just under two days' pay for the trip. Conductors in 1976 averaged $27,500 per year and brakemen $26,500.[28] There are no analogous employees on a bus.

The on-board service crew of Amtrak employees consisted of a head waiter and two service attendants, all of whom were paid on an hourly basis under a union contract that guaranteed 180 hours of pay per month. Other costs shown in table 14 are as billed by Conrail or allocated among Amtrak's trains using the facilities generally. The train used Amtrak's owned trackage between Michigan City and Kalamazoo.

[26] "Should Amtrak Develop High-Speed Corridor Service outside the Northeast?" General Accounting Office, Report no. CED–78–67 (1978), p. 21.
[27] Report from the American Bus Association, 1977, p. 29.
[28] "Should Amtrak Develop High-Speed Corridor Service outside the Northeast?" p. 21.

TABLE 15
Energy Efficiency of Carriers, 1976

Carrier	Passenger-Mile Market Share (percent)	Load Factor (percent)	Btus per Passenger-Mile	Passenger-Miles per Gallon	Btus per Passenger-Mile at 100% Load
Automobile	87.2	46.3[a]	2,837	44.0	1,314
Air	11.2	58.6	5,052	26.7	2,960
Bus	1.3	44.0	1,075	129.1	473
Rail	0.3	45.0	3,123	44.4	1,405

[a] Calculated on basis of average seating capacity of 5.62 and average intercity occupancy of 2.6.
Source: U.S. Congress, Senate, *Report to Accompany S. 712, Amtrak Improvement Act of 1979*, Calendar no. 194, Report no. 96–183, 96th Congress, 1st session (1979), p. 4.

The GAO, which had previously expressed satisfaction with Amtrak's cost-accounting techniques, concluded that, given the constraints of the union contracts, cost reductions were unlikely except possibly in the area of car maintenance. Consequently, the pecuniary costs of train 355 may be taken as approximately representative of the actual costs, in an economist's sense, of transporting people by train within current constraints. To break even, Amtrak would have had to charge Chicago–Detroit passengers $29.80, whereas its fare was $20.50. Bus fare was $21.40 and air fare $40.00. The GAO estimated the average total cost of operating an automobile from Detroit to Chicago at $47.43 and the marginal cost at $13.95.[29]

Comparisons with Rival Carriers

Fuel Efficiency. The passenger train is a large, heavy vehicle, which requires continual acceleration and deceleration, and therefore heavy energy inputs. As table 15 demonstrates, intercity passenger trains require just over half the fuel per passenger-mile of aircraft, slightly more than automobiles, and nearly triple that of buses. The document from which the table was taken comments:

> The average Amtrak train in fiscal year 1978 carried 128 passengers. Amtrak would have to average over 138 pas-

---

[29] Ibid., p. 12.

sengers to compete with an average automobile and over 400 passengers to compete with the bus industry. Furthermore, in the event of a national energy emergency, the simple fact is that Amtrak does not have the equipment or manpower to handle significantly higher ridership levels.[30]

Amtrak itself has reported to the House Appropriations Committee that it would have to handle 143 passengers per train to equal automobiles in energy efficiency and 420 to equal busses.[31] As recently as 1978 the corporation expressed optimism that it could approximate the fuel efficiency of intercity buses with its electrically heated Amfleet equipment,[32] but in 1979 it reported to the Appropriations Committee:

> With existing conditions, rail is far from a favorable comparison with intercity bus from the standpoint of energy efficiency. While new lightweight equipment, an emphasis on short-haul corridor operations, and greater use of electric trains in the Northeast Corridor will surely increase Amtrak's overall energy efficiency, equality with bus will seldom be achieved, if ever, on long distance routes, barring a technological breakthrough in railroading.[33]

Safety. Amtrak provides an extremely safe form of transportation, with a fatality rate a third that of bus and a sixth that of air (table 16). Rail passenger service has always had this attraction, but it did not prevent the decline of demand. If society has for about forty years depended on the automobile for 85 to 90 percent of intercity movements, it appears that accident risks far higher than those of any common carrier are tolerable to the majority. Indeed, it is not apparently rational to consider the relative accident experience of the three common carriers if one is willing to accept the risks of automobile travel at all.

Speed and Punctuality. Many studies of the railroads' decline have noted that their major competitive disadvantage for freight is the high

---

[30] U.S. Congress, Senate, *Report to Accompany S. 712, Amtrak Improvement Act of 1979*, Calendar no. 194, Report no. 96–183, 96th Congress, 1st session (1979), p. 4.

[31] U.S. Congress, House of Representatives, *Department of Transportation and Related Agencies Appropriations for 1980*, Hearings before a Subcommittee of the Committee on Appropriations, 96th Congress, 1st session (1979) (hereafter cited as House Appropriations Hearing, 1980), p. 842.

[32] House Appropriations Hearing, 1979, p. 890.

[33] House Appropriations Hearing, 1980, p. 842.

TABLE 16
FATALITIES PER 10 BILLION PASSENGER-MILES, AMTRAK AND RIVAL CARRIERS

Carrier	Fatalities
Bus	3
Amtrak	1
Automobile	140
Airlines	6

SOURCE: House Appropriations Hearing, 1979, p. 886.

variance in arrival times relative to highway transport.[34] Because Amtrak still uses railroads' right-of-way, and these still serve mainly freight, it is impossible to avoid punctuality problems. Further, the demand for rail passenger service is highly concentrated in the Northeast where the railroads are oldest, built with earliest engineering standards, and set in some of the most difficult terrain. In recent years, the northeastern railroads have been the most depressed, and consequently the most deteriorated.

Railroading has the odd property that dynamic problems in freight train operation are worst at intermediate speeds: the 39-foot interval of rail joints tends to augment the natural frequency with which cars sway at speeds between 10 and 30 miles per hour. This causes highly deteriorated track to become unsafe at very moderate speeds, and thus subject to 10-mile-per-hour slow orders.[35] In consequence, Amtrak is unable to provide even the standards of speed and punctuality of the railroads in the fairly recent past, much less the standards of its present rivals. Amtrak's *Broadway Limited* via the former Pennsylvania Railroad main line requires about twenty hours to provide a trip made for many years at a standard sixteen-hour schedule. When Amtrak restored service between Washington and Cincinnati on the Baltimore & Ohio's St. Louis line, it required two hours and fifteen minutes longer westbound and three hours longer eastbound than the B&O's steam locomotives took in the early 1950s.[36]

---

[34] For example, Kenneth Boyer, "Minimum Rate Regulation, Modal Split Sensitivities, and the Railroad Problem," *Journal of Political Economy*, vol. 85 (1977), pp. 493–512.

[35] See George W. Hilton, *The Northeast Railroad Problem* (Washington, D.C.: American Enterprise Institute, 1975), pp. 16–21.

[36] *Trains*, August 1976, p. 9.

Public policy aggravated the problem by providing a reward for punctuality that proved to inhibit speed. The incentive agreements Amtrak began including in its contracts with the railroads on July 1, 1974, provided for bonuses to the railroads for schedule adherence, making up lost time en route, schedule improvement, and equipment availability, as measured by promptness in maintenance or repair. Penalties were provided for excessive delays of trains on the road and for substandard cleanliness of cars at the start of runs. Equipment operability, defined as operation on the line without failure, could bring either an incentive payment or a penalty.

The GAO studied the first two years' experience of the incentive program and found that some 95 percent of its net expenditure was for schedule adherence on a continuing basis (see table 17). The reward for schedule improvement was a one-time payment, which no railroad saw fit to secure, while ten received payments for adherence. Consequently, such effect as the program had was almost entirely in securing adherence to published schedules. Not surprisingly, the railroads responded to this incentive structure by modifying schedules to make them easier to observe. Amtrak's average speed fell from 51.5 miles per hour in 1971 to just over 45 miles per hour in 1977.[37]

On January 1, 1974, just before the incentive contracts began, Amtrak modified its definition of punctuality. Previously, a train was considered late if it arrived at its terminus more than five minutes behind schedule. Thereafter, Amtrak used a sliding scale, interpreting "on time" as being up to five minutes late for trips up to 150 miles, but within thirty minutes for trips of 551 miles or more. Since punctuality was measured only at the final destination, the railroads typically inserted "cushions" in the schedules approaching the termini so that time could readily be made up. The effect was to reduce punctuality at intermediate points.

Even with the relaxed standard of on-time performance, Amtrak suffered a decline in punctuality. In 1974 about 75 percent of Amtrak's trains were on time, but in 1977 only 62 percent were.[38] The corporation attributed the problem, and also the deterioration of its speeds, mainly to poor track. Amtrak's officials believe that its trains must provide service at least at the legal highway speed of 55 miles per hour to be competitive with its surface rivals.

Amtrak initially implemented the incentive program by establishing a benchmark, usually 65 percent, for on-time arrivals, above which

[37] "Should Amtrak Develop High-Speed Corridor Service outside the Northeast?" p. 15.
[38] Ibid., p. 16.

TABLE 17

Amtrak Net Incentive Payments (Penalties) to June, 1976

Incentive Category	Dollar Amount
Schedule adherence	32,598,297
Recovered time and excessive delays	64,285
Schedule improvement	0
Car cleanliness	(23,950)
Equipment operability	356,061
Equipment availability	1,197,005
Total	34,191,698

Source: "Amtrak's Incentive Contracts with Railroads—Considerable Costs, Few Benefits," General Accounting Office, Report no. CED–77–69 (1977), p. 5.

benefits were paid and below which penalties were levied. This method, in view of the freedom to relax the schedule and the liberalized definition of "on time," gave rise to several anomalies. The following are quoted from the GAO study of the incentive program:

> During July 1974 through December 1975 Milwaukee Road trains were on time 89.6 percent of the time. For this, Milwaukee Road received a bonus of $2.2 million. Using the old 5-minute criteria—no schedule changes were made— on-time performance would have been 84 percent, or approximately the same level experienced by Milwaukee Road before the incentive contract. Thus, no performance increase was achieved for the $2.2 million.
>
> The Burlington Northern received $2.7 million for having 85.8 percent of its trains arrive on time from July through December 1974. On the surface, this is a substantial improvement over 58 percent on-time performance for the same period in 1973. However, using the current criteria the on-time arrival for the 1973 period would have been 82.4 percent. Therefore, a 3.4 percent increase in performance cost $2.7 million.
>
> The Southern Pacific received $3.7 million in on-time performance incentives for December 1974 through June 1976. Southern Pacific's on-time performance was approximately 81 percent before and after the incentive contract. If Amtrak had not changed the arrival criteria, the on-time performance would have been 74 percent under the incentive contract. Thus, Amtrak paid $3.7 million for decreased performance.
>
> The Seaboard Coast Line received $11.8 million for 94.4 percent on-time performance from September 1974 through

June 1976. Although this performance represents a substantial increase over the 70 percent performance experienced in 1973, the increase was due primarily to a change in arrival criteria and very loose schedules rather than improved performance.[39]

Recognizing these shortcomings, Amtrak moved in 1977 to a new incentive system, the so-called "second amendment" agreements with the railroads. These contracts set the base for punctuality at 80 percent and made an effort to tie the incentive payments to the actual costs of punctuality or lack of it to the railroads involved.[40] The subsequent experience has not yet been evaluated.

Amtrak's goal of 80 percent schedule adherence is itself a demonstration of the impossibility of providing a high degree of punctuality in a service that mixes passenger and freight trains. Air transport is between 75 and 85 percent punctual, defined as arriving within fifteen minutes of scheduled time.[41] Bus lines do not publish punctuality figures, but Greyhound informally estimates on the basis of overtime claims in payrolls that its operations are approximately 85 percent punctual, interpreted as arrival at destination within ten minutes of schedule.[42] Similarly, Amtrak's target of 55 miles per hour overall is merely the legal free-running speed of buses on the interstate freeway system, which rivals virtually all Amtrak trains. This, it hardly need be added, is an artificial constraint on buses, dependent on public policy. Previously, in 1973, the average operating speed of American buses had been 60.4 miles per hour, an improvement of 20 percent over 1950.[43]

Frequency. Amtrak's basic network provides service by a single train per day with the exception of the northeast and midwest corridor services, the New York–Miami trains, and the Los Angeles–San Diego trains. As the railroads had concluded, losses are minimized by concentrating the remaining ridership on a single train. Given the cost inferiority of rail service to buses, providing frequency to rival the bus operations is unbearably costly; it can be attempted only in the northeast corridor. Even in the Chicago–Milwaukee corridor,

[39] "Amtrak's Incentive Contracts with Railroads—Considerable Costs, Few Benefits," General Accounting Office, Report no. CED–77–69 (1977), pp. 12–13.

[40] Ibid., p. 17.

[41] Frank C. Mulvey, *Amtrak: An Experiment in Rail Service*, National Transportation Policy Study Commission, Report no. NTPSC/SR–78/02 (1978), p. 105.

[42] Interview with Nicholas E. Bade, director of marketing, Greyhound Lines, July 18, 1978.

[43] Mulvey, *Amtrak: An Experiment in Rail Service*, p. 114.

TABLE 18
Amtrak's Financial Experience, 1971–1978
(thousands of dollars)

Fiscal Year	Operating Revenue	Operating Expense	Deficit	Revenue as Percentage of Expense
1971	22,645	45,301	22,656	50.0
1972	152,709	306,179	153,470	49.9
1973	177,303	319,151	141,848	55.6
1974	240,071	437,932	197,861	54.8
1975	246,549	559,807	313,348	44.0
1976	268,038	674,307	406,269	39.8
Transition quarter	77,167	176,298	99,131	43.7
1977	311,272	832,850	521,578	37.4
1978	313,002	856,598	543,596	36.5
Total	1,808,666	4,208,423	2,499,757	

Sources: "Should Amtrak Develop High-Speed Corridor Service outside the Northeast?" General Accounting Office, Report CED–78–67 (1978), p. 2; "Four Years of Amtrak Operation," updated unpublished Department of Transportation study, Amtrak Annual Report, 1978, p. 30.

where Amtrak provides relatively dense service, it operates only six trains in each direction, in rivalry with twenty daily Greyhound buses. Between Chicago and Detroit, Amtrak operates four runs and Greyhound ten.[44] Given the high value placed on frequency, demonstrated in the regression presented earlier, Amtrak's inferiority to bus and other rivals in this dimension is one of its worst handicaps.

Comprehensiveness. Amtrak's route system of some 26,000 miles served 512 stations in 1976.[45] As of October 1976, 40 of these— mostly small towns in the Northwest—were served by no other form of public transportation.[46] In contrast, the intercity bus system in the same year covered 276,000 miles of route serving more than 15,000 communities, of which over 14,000 had no other form of public transportation.[47] The scheduled airlines served 485 airports.[48] As

[44] *Russell's Official National Motor Coach Guide*, May 1979; *The Official Railway Guide*, May 1979.

[45] *Background on Amtrak*, (Washington, D.C.: National Railroad Passenger Corporation, 1977), p. 27.

[46] "Should Amtrak Develop High-Speed Corridor Service outside the Northeast?" p. 26.

[47] *Report from the American Bus Association*, p. 4.

[48] *Amtrak Yesterday, Today, and Tomorrow*, Figure 13.

TABLE 19

FEDERAL FINANCING OF AMTRAK, 1971–1978
(millions of dollars)

Fiscal Year	Operating Grants	Guaranteed Loan Authority	Direct Capital Grants
1971	40.0	100.0	—
1972–73	179.1	100.0	—
1974	140.0	300.0	—
1975	278.0	400.0	—
1976	357.0	—	114.2
Transition quarter	105.0	—	25.0
1977	482.6	—	93.1
1978	536.0	—	157.0
Total	2,117.7	900.0	388.3

SOURCES: *Background on Amtrak* (Washington, D.C.: National Railroad Passenger Corporation, 1977), p. 11; Amtrak Annual Report, 1978, p. 30.

with schedule frequency, the adverse costs of rail passenger service made rivalry with the bus network's comprehensiveness impossible. The inherent constraints of the mode made rivalry with airlines in speed impossible.

Financial Experience

Amtrak's operating experience is consistent with an unsatisfactory and steadily worsening financial experience. The corporation's financial performance over its history shows deficits increasing both absolutely and relative to revenue (see table 18). At the outset, the service covered approximately half its costs from revenues, but after a temporary improvement at the time of the oil shortage–induced increase in ridership, this figure had fallen to only 37.4 percent by 1977. Losses per passenger and per passenger-mile show a similar trend. As a result, Amtrak has required an extensive operating subsidy.

The corporation's initial statutory authority provided for an operating grant of $40 million and guaranteed loan authority for capital improvement of $100 million. Table 19 shows this and subsequent experience. The guaranteed loan authority proved unsuitable for a chronically unprofitable enterprise and was replaced in fiscal 1976 by direct capital grants, mainly for purchase of the electrically heated cars and second-generation diesel locomotives. State financial

TABLE 20

TRANSPORTATION SUBSIDIES AS A PERCENTAGE OF
EXPENDITURES BY USERS, FISCAL YEARS 1974–1976

	1974	1975	1976
Air transportation			
Air carrier[a]	1	1	1
General aviation[b]	12	13	14
Highway transportation[c]			1
Railroad transportation			
Passenger[d]	54	82	113
Freight[e]	1	2	3
Water transportation			
International freight[f]	8	10	11
U.S.–Flag only	29	37	41
Domestic freight[g]	21	22	21
Inland only	47	44	41
Mass transportation[h]	49	54	73

[a] The subsidy includes a portion of the Federal Aviation Administration's expenditures plus the subsidy to local service air carriers administered by the Civil Aeronautics Board. FAA expenditures and excise tax revenue were allocated between air carriers and general aviation on the basis of the Department of Transportation's 1973 cost allocation study. Air carrier revenue data for 1974 is from U.S. Department of Transportation, *Summary of National Transportation Statistics*, June 1976 (hereafter, *DOT-Statistics*); 1975 revenue is from U.S. Department of Transportation, *National Transportation Trends and Choices*, January 1977 (hereafter, *DOT-Trends*).

[b] Includes allocated FAA expenditures. General aviation expenditure data are from *DOT-Statistics* in 1974 and *DOT-Trends* in 1975.

[c] There was a negative subsidy in 1974 and 1975, since revenues exceeded expenditures.

[d] Includes grants to Amtrak as well as the principal of federal guaranteed loans. Revenue data are from American Association of Railroads, *Yearbook of Railroad Facts*, 1976 (hereafter, *Railroad Facts*).

[e] ConRail security purchases are not included; they were $309,000,000 in fiscal year 1976. Revenue data are from *Railroad Facts*.

[f] Includes the various subsidies from the Maritime Administration plus a portion of corps expenditures for deep draft channels and harbors. Revenue data are from discussions with the Bureau of Economic Analysis, U.S. Department of Commerce.

[g] Revenue data are from *DOT-Statistics* in 1974 and *DOT-Trends* in 1975.

[h] Includes the various subsidies from the Urban Mass Transportation Administration plus federal aid to Washington, D.C., subway. Revenue data are from American Public Transit Association, *Transit Fact Book* (1975–1976 edition).

SOURCE: House Appropriations Hearing, 1979, p. 881.

support is relatively small, amounting to about $1.5 million per year for subsidy of the section 403(b) services.

This level of federal funding makes Amtrak the most heavily subsidized form of American transportation, measured by public subvention relative to expenditure by users. Table 20 is a tabulation by the Congressional Budget Office of subsidies as a percentage of users' expenditures. An Amtrak passenger enjoys a subsidy greater than an urban transit passenger, the next most highly subsidized user, by nearly two-thirds. Since by Amtrak's own estimates, the deficit will reach $876 million by 1982,[49] the problem of Amtrak's finances will require more careful attention than Congress has given it to date.

---

[49] "An Analysis of Amtrak's Five Year Plan," General Accounting Office, Report no. PAD-78-51 (1978).

4
Evaluation of the Amtrak Program

The Amtrak experiment has been unsuccessful by any standards. If patronage of railroad passenger trains of 1950 presented the target for attainment, achieved levels of ridership represent only about a fifth of the goal. As table 21 demonstrates, Amtrak trains annually provided under a third of 1 percent of intercity passenger-miles between 1971 and 1976, with relatively low variance per year. Such minor decline in the degree of automobile dependence as the country showed in the period resulted mainly from the absolute and relative expansion of air travel.

Under the circumstances, such external benefits as the trains produced could only have been minor, or conversely, such external benefits as the system generated were produced at a cost that would not ordinarily be considered justified. This generalization is consistent with the conclusions of a recent federal study of Amtrak by Frank P. Mulvey for the National Transportation Policy Study Commission.

Professor Mulvey attempted to quantify Amtrak's external benefits on the basis of the trains' reported diversion of passengers from alternative modes of intercity transport. For safety, he concluded that Amtrak's diversion from automobiles resulted in saving of thirty-three lives in 1976, with a consequent benefit of $10 million to $33 million, plus other benefits in safety of $18 million for a total of $28 to $51 million.[1] For fuel saving, if Amtrak's reported diversion from automobiles were carried in Amfleet equipment, the annual saving would amount to 53 million gallons for a benefit calculated at $29.2 million. This represents an upper limit, for not all passengers are carried in Amfleet cars. There is a further matter that if Amtrak's

---

[1] Frank C. Mulvey, *Amtrak: An Experiment in Rail Service*, National Transportation Policy Study Commission, Report no. NTPSC/SR–78/02 (1978), p. 105.

TABLE 21
Distribution of Intercity Travel between Private and Public Carriers, 1972–1978
(billions of passenger-miles)

Types of Carriers	1972	1973	1974	1975	1976	1977	1978
Private carriers							
Automobile							
No.	1,129.0	1,166.3	1,070.7	1,123.2	1,213.1	1,245.9	1,304.5
%	87.1	86.7	85.3	86.0	85.9	85.4	84.6
Air							
No.	10.0	10.7	10.8	11.1	11.6	12.1	12.7
%	0.8	0.8	0.9	0.8	0.8	0.8	0.8
Total private							
No.	1,139.0	1,177.0	1,081.5	1,134.3	1,224.7	1,258.0	1,317.2
%	87.9	87.5	86.2	86.8	86.7	86.2	85.4
Public carriers							
Air							
No.	123.0	132.4	135.4	136.9	152.3	164.2	189.1
%	9.5	9.8	10.8	10.5	10.8	11.3	12.3
Bus							
No.	25.6	26.4	27.7	25.4	25.1	25.7	25.4
%	1.9	2.0	2.2	1.9	1.8	1.8	1.6
Railroad							
Non-Amtrak[a]							
No.	5.7	5.5	6.2	6.2	6.2	6.1	6.4
%	0.46	0.41	0.47	0.49	0.42	0.41	0.43
Amtrak							
No.	3.0	3.8	4.3	3.9	4.2	4.3	4.1
%	0.24	0.29	0.33	0.31	0.28	0.29	0.27
Total public							
No.	157.3	168.1	173.6	172.4	187.8	200.3	225.0
%	12.1	12.5	13.8	13.2	13.3	13.8	14.6
Total intercity travel	1,296.3	1,345.1	1,255.1	1,306.7	1,412.5	1,458.3	1,542.2

[a] Includes commutation.

Source: Transportation Association of America; table 2, above.

ridership were diverted to bus, the saving would be much greater. By way of contrast, Mulvey pointed out that rigorous enforcement of the 55 miles-per-hour speed limit would save 2.5 billion gallons of gasoline per year.[2]

---

[2] Ibid., pp. 71–73.

For pollution, Mulvey estimated that Amtrak reduced the output of carbon dioxide by 54,320 tons and of hydrocarbons by 4,497 tons per year, but increased output of nitrogen oxides by 9,433 tons, of sulphur oxides by 1,724 tons, and particulates by 130 tons per year. These figures, whether representing increases or decreases, are infinitesimal relative to the total national output. In 1972 emission from stationary sources of nitrogen oxides was 11.7 million tons and of hydrocarbons, 27.1 million tons.[3]

Any benefits of reduction of air congestion which Amtrak produces are necessarily in the northeast corridor. At $10 per minute operating cost of aircraft and 10 cents per minute valuation of travelers' time, Mulvey estimated the benefits of air passenger diversion in the corridor at slightly over $1.5 million.[4] Diversion from automobiles, he estimated, reduces automobile traffic in the northeast corridor by about 2 percent, but the resultant savings in time of $10-to-25 million are so widely diffused as to be barely perceptible.[5] Adversely, he estimates the loss of road and airport user charges from Amtrak's existence at $6.1 million.[6] He made no firm estimates on noise.

Direct measures, Professor Mulvey pointed out, would have been uniformly more effective. The reduction in emissions of hydrocarbons and nitrogen oxides attributed to Amtrak's northeast corridor and short-distance services could be produced by more stringent standards for automobile emissions for about $4.1 million. Improvement in utility boilers could reduce nitrogen oxide emissions for a marginal cost of about $100 per ton.[7] Amtrak's losses—on the order of a half billion dollars per year—cannot be justified by its external benefits, given the relative economy of direct measures. Mulvey noted that in spite of the well-publicized inefficiencies of regulated air transport, the average cost of moving air passengers in 1974 was about 8 cents per revenue passenger-mile, which was less than Amtrak's deficit. Thus, the government could have moved them by air for the public money spent on Amtrak and produced the external benefits more economically by direct measures.[8]

A benefit widely claimed for Amtrak, but not treated by Professor Mulvey, is provision of surplus capacity which is useful in emergency situations. Amtrak's ridership rose about 20 percent as a consequence of the oil shortage of 1973–1974. In 1979 a renewed oil shortage, a

[3] Ibid., pp. 80–81.
[4] Ibid., p. 88.
[5] Ibid., p. 92.
[6] Ibid., p. 93.
[7] Ibid., p. 82.
[8] Ibid., p. 141.

major strike against United Airlines, and the grounding of DC–10 aircraft combined to make alternatives more costly. The consequence was again to increase Amtrak's ridership by about 20 percent. Unfortunately, Amtrak's percentage of all intercity movements is so low that the marginal significance of such increases is negligible. Amtrak estimates that if increased demand raised its load factors from its customary 45 percent to 75 percent, annual ridership would rise from about 19 million to 27 million.[9] An increase of this magnitude would still leave Amtrak hauling less than half of 1 percent of intercity travelers. Even tripling Amtrak's output would still fall short of 1 percent of intercity movements. In the 1973–1974 oil shortage, the absolute increase in ridership of the intercity bus industry was more than triple Amtrak's increase. Buses, which operate at load factors similar to Amtrak's, 44 percent in 1976, can deal with exceptional increases in demand more easily because of their greater frequency and comprehensiveness of service.

Amtrak's failure stems directly from the logic whereby the corporation was established. As pointed out in chapter 1, the decline of the passenger train was subject to two interpretations. The first, as exemplified in the Hosmer Report, attributed it mainly to passengers' valuation of time and to the costs of the passenger train relative to its rivals. The second, as exemplified by Peter Lyon's *To Hell in a Day Coach*, saw it as the result of an effort by the railroads to discourage use of the trains by downgrading the quality of service. Amtrak's experience has shown that the Hosmer Report was right and the discouragement hypothesis is fallacious. The system has manifested relatively high price elasticities of demand outside the northeast corridor, a high cross-elasticity of demand with buses, and a high sensitivity of quantity demanded to frequency, but little evidence of high responsiveness to the quality of service. First-class travel has continued its secular decline relative to coach, and the luxury aspects of rail travel have continued to be unprofitable.

Indeed, much of what has been unsatisfactory in Amtrak's performance resulted from the effort to restore ridership by improving the quality of service. Food and beverage service, which produces about 7 percent of Amtrak's revenue, is highly unprofitable, as it was for the railroads. In 1977 food and beverage service produced $21.3 million in revenue for Amtrak at a cost of $63.8 million, a $42.5 million loss.[10] In addition, dining cars and lounge cars are nonrevenue equip-

---

[9] House Appropriations Hearing, 1980, p. 852.

[10] "Amtrak's Subsidy Needs Cannot Be Reduced without Reducing Service," General Accounting Office, Report no. CED–78–86 (1978), p. 19.

ment, housing no passengers but adding to the weight of the trains. They are in part responsible for Amtrak's poor energy efficiency relative to its rivals. Similarly, sleeping cars are heavier than coaches, but have lower passenger capacities. Amtrak's hopes for equaling the energy efficiency of buses are based on use of Amfleet coaches with relatively dense seating capacities and on limited buffet facilities. In parallel fashion, dining cars, lounges, and sleeping cars are all more labor-intensive than coaches.

Amtrak is empowered to carry mail and express, but such revenues have run to only about 7 percent of its receipts—approximately the same as food and beverages. The Postal Service shows no tendency to reverse its long-range program of diversion of mails to other modes, which is now virtually complete. Consequently, Amtrak finds itself operating trains with heavy labor and fuel costs but small head-end revenues—exactly the sort of train that was most unprofitable during railroad operations.

Given the losses associated with the luxury aspects of rail travel, an effort to restore ridership by increasing the quality of service aggravated the actual problem. It should have been apparent at the outset that the effort was bound to fail. The massive replacement of conventional equipment with streamlined equipment between 1946 and 1952 had not enabled the passenger train to compete with automobiles and buses on conventional roads or with piston aircraft. The buses and automobiles now have the interstate freeway system as right-of-way, and the airlines have been reequipped with jet aircraft, while railroad rights-of-way, especially in the Northeast where the demand is highly concentrated, have deteriorated seriously. More generally, the effort to provide a high quality of service puts Amtrak in rivalry with cruise ships, resort hotels, and a variety of other enterprises that do not have the constraints of a moving vehicle with a steel-on-steel contact with its right-of-way. The quality of service that this mode of transportation is inherently capable of providing is typically grossly overstated.[11]

The effort to restore ridership by enhancing the quality of service was in some part responsible for Amtrak's rapid escalation of costs. Other reasons suggested have been the growth of Amtrak's office staff, inflationary pressures, and the general problems of operating

---

[11] "The most sensible way of traveling between cities a few hundred miles apart, the most efficient way, the cheapest, the most convenient, the surest, the safest, potentially the most comfortable, the easiest, and the best way, is the way that has been available for a hundred years or more; in short, the railway." [Peter Lyon, *To Hell in a Day Coach* (New York: Lippincott, 1968), p. 226.]

an aged car fleet. The General Accounting Office has suggested a specific study of the increase in Amtrak's costs, but it has provisionally concluded on the basis of its existing studies that the corporation is generally operated efficiently. It cannot significantly reduce its need for subsidy without reducing its system.[12]

The high level of costs, in turn, prevents the frequency in scheduling that would make Amtrak a comprehensively effective rival to the bus industry. Only in the northeast corridor has Amtrak provided frequency to match what the bus industry provides in most populous areas. In lightly populated areas, it is typically impracticable to offer Amtrak service as a rival to buses at all. Finally, only between New York and Washington can Amtrak provide schedules that are at all air-competitive.

Impact on Rival Carriers

Even though Amtrak provides less than 0.5 percent of American intercity trips, its existence necessarily affects rival carriers. In the markets where it operates, Amtrak reports about an 18 percent share of common carrier passengers.[13] In the northeast corridor, where trains provide about 12 percent of intercity trips of all sorts, Amtrak has achieved about 40 percent of air-and-train traffic between New York and Washington.[14] Such impact as Amtrak has on rival carriers is manifested mainly in the northeast corridor.

Amtrak's impact on the airlines is thought to be almost entirely in the northeast corridor. Elsewhere, Amtrak's passenger counts are too small relative either to the airlines' absolute passenger volumes or to their rate of traffic growth for the effect to be significant. In any case, Amtrak's short average distance assures that most of its passengers would be bus-competitive. In the northeast corridor, the New York–Washington distance of 226 miles is short enough for trains to be air-competitive for people with an average valuation of time. The most authoritative recent study of valuation of time implies that the break between surface and air as the optimal mode is around 176 miles.[15] Further, the nature of Amtrak's physical plant plus some

[12] "Amtrak's Subsidy Needs Cannot Be Reduced without Reducing Service."

[13] U.S. Congress, House of Representatives, *Department of Transportation and Related Agencies Appropriations for 1978*, Hearings before a Subcommittee of the Committee on Appropriations, 95th Congress, 1st session (1977) (hereafter cited as House Appropriations Hearing, 1978), p. 483.

[14] *Two Year Report on the Northeast Corridor*, Department of Transportation, February 1978, p. 3; House Appropriations Hearing, 1979, p. 891.

[15] Reuben Gronau, *The Value of Time in Passenger Transportation*, Occasional Paper no. 109 (New York: National Bureau of Economic Research, 1970).

other geographical considerations permit trains to be more nearly competitive in time with air between New York and Washington than anywhere else.

The federal government's efforts to improve rail service between the two cities antedates Amtrak. A separate Northeast Corridor Project, subsequently incorporated into Amtrak, introduced the Metroliners, geared to operate at 160 miles per hour, in 1968. Operations at these speeds proved impractical on tracks used by freight and other passenger trains, but the cars ultimately proved capable of providing the service in approximately three hours and twenty minutes. Amtrak has largely refitted the conventional trains with Amfleet equipment; they provide the service in somewhat over four hours. The Metroliners are priced for the longer distances at about 10.9 cents per mile with a net loss of 5.6 cents per mile. The conventional trains are priced about 9.0 cents per mile with a net loss of 10.8 cents per mile. Rival air fares are approximately 16.3 cents per mile.[16]

Figure 1 illustrates the respective trends in ridership. The Eastern Airlines shuttle has lost ridership absolutely. By 1976 the refurbished conventional trains had surpassed the Metroliners in ridership, and together trains provided nearly as many trips as the shuttle. (There are air passengers between the two cities other than on the shuttle.) Eastern was of the opinion until about 1975 that its shuttle services cross-subsidized the rest of its system. Its present view is that subsequent de facto deregulation of air transport has probably ended any significant cross-subsidy. Eastern has no current estimate of loss in revenue as a consequence of the existence of its subsidized rival.[17]

Inevitably, Amtrak's impact on the bus industry is much greater, although the exact magnitude is unclear. The characteristics of Amtrak's passengers, the speeds at which it operates, and the length of its typical haul all produce a higher marginal rate of substitution with bus service than with air. There are enough restrictions on exit from bus operation on the state level that cross-subsidization of minor routes by main lines is thought present in the bus industry, and, unlike the airlines, the bus industry has historically had a declining rate of output and a shrinking route mileage. There is abundant evidence that Amtrak's existence has increased the bus transport industry's rate of decline.

Amtrak has an unregulated fare structure and operates under heavy subsidy. Its fares rise at about two-thirds the rate of inflation.

---

[16] House Appropriations Hearing, 1979, pp. 885–965.

[17] Letter to the author of James E. Reinke, vice-president for government affairs, Eastern Airlines, August 9, 1978.

FIGURE 1
New York—Washington, D.C., Rail and Air Shuttle Passengers, 1960—1976

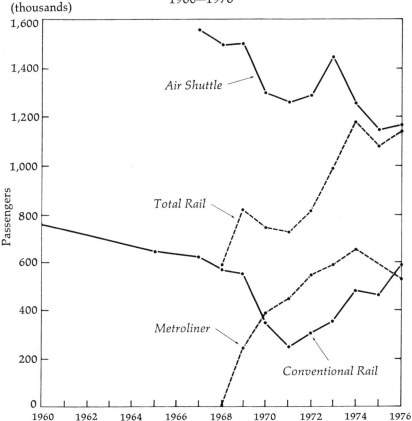

Source: Robert L. Winestone, "Staff Paper: Ten Years of Train-Air Data in the New York to Washington Passenger Market," Department of Transportation, Federal Railroad Administration, Office of Federal Assistance, Rail Passenger Programs Division, May 1977.

Given relatively high elasticities of demand and considerable political pressure for a show of expanding ridership, the corporation has an incentive to narrow the differences between rail and bus fares. Because of the subsidy, costs provide no constraint on this policy. On the basis of a sample of rates on routes that directly compete with Amtrak, Greyhound reported to the House Committee on Interstate and Foreign Commerce that Amtrak's one-way fares had fallen from 25.9 percent above bus in February 1972 to 1.1 percent above bus in February 1978 (see table 22). The figure for round-trip and excursion fares is more

69

TABLE 22

A Comparison of Typical Intercity Bus and Amtrak One-Way Fares, 1972 and 1978

	January 16, 1972		February 10, 1978	
	Bus	Amtrak	Bus	Amtrak
New York, N.Y.–				
Boston, Mass.	$10.45	$12.75	$20.40	$19.50
Philadelphia, Pa.	4.85	5.25	9.40	9.25
Washington, D.C.	11.20	13.00	20.95	20.50
Pittsburgh, Pa.	19.10	25.25	33.85	33.00
Miami, Fla.	52.45	59.01	88.30	86.00
Buffalo, N.Y.	19.40	22.75	36.10	34.40
Chicago, Ill.	36.40	51.25	64.30	56.00
Chicago, Ill.–				
St. Louis, Mo.	11.05	13.50	19.55	19.50
Kansas City, Mo.	18.75	17.00	33.20	32.50
Milkwaukee, Wis.	3.70	4.00	6.55	6.25
Minneapolis, Minn.	13.25	17.50	23.45	32.50
Detroit, Mich.	12.70	16.25	22.45	20.50
Cincinnati, Ohio	13.80	17.00	24.40	20.50
New Orleans, La.	31.90	45.00	56.40	54.00
New Orleans, La.–				
Memphis, Tenn.	18.75	19.00	33.20	30.00
Los Angeles, Calif.–				
San Diego, Calif.	4.63	4.75	7.48	9.00
San Francisco, Calif.	13.56	21.00	21.72	26.50
Phoenix. Ariz.	15.95	19.25	28.25	33.00
Seattle, Wash.	38.50	57.25	68.20	80.00
Seattle, Wash.–				
Portland, Oreg.	5.40	6.75	9.60	11.75

	Bus	Amtrak	% Amtrak Greater or Less than Bus
Average one-way fare			
1972	$17.78	$22.38	+25.9
1978	31.39	31.73	+ 1.1
Percent increase	76.5	42.0	
Average round-trip or excursion fare			
1972	$32.95	$41.12	+24.8
1978	50.65	44.98	−11.2
Percent increase	53.7	9.4	

SOURCE: Submission of Greyhound Corporation to House Committee on Interstate and Foreign Commerce, April 3, 1978, based on Bus and Amtrak tariffs deposited with ICC.

TABLE 23

CLASS I CARRIERS' INCOME, 1971–1976

(dollars in millions)

Year	Number of Carriers	Net Operating Revenue[a]	Net Income[b]	Return on Equity[c]
1971	71	$94.9	$64.5	16.1%
1972	74	85.7	58.9	14.7
1973	75	76.6	54.6	13.7
1974	81	73.9	56.1	13.3
1975	77	61.1	56.4	12.5
1976	76	44.2	38.6	8.3

[a] The term "net operating revenue" (operating revenue less operating expenses) is almost synonymous with the term "net carrier operating income."
[b] Net income includes fixed charges, nonoperating income, income taxes, and extraordinary and prior-period items.
[c] Net income divided by average of beginning and end-of-year stockholders' equity.
SOURCE: *The Intercity Bus Industry: A Preliminary Study*, Interstate Commerce Commission, Bureau of Economics, May 1978.

extreme: Amtrak's fare levels for these services went from 24.8 percent above bus to 11.2 percent below over the same time period. This fare policy had two inevitable consequences: first, it accelerated the rate of decline of bus ridership; second, it damped the rate of increase of bus fares in response to inflation.

It is indisputable that a marked worsening in the position of the bus industry coincided with the establishment of Amtrak in 1971, but it is not clear how far Amtrak is responsible for the situation. As tables 23–27 demonstrate, Class I motor carriers suffered a decline of net operating revenues of over 50 percent from 1971 to 1976, a decline of net income of about 40 percent, and a decline of return of equity of about half. Passenger counts fell some 17 percent and route mileage 13 percent. Greyhound Lines, the industry's dominant firm, expects to be in the red by 1980.

The bus industry's recent decline in ridership is highly concentrated in regular-route intercity service (see table 25). Local and special services have declined only at rates approximating the industry's previous secular decline. The bus industry is of the opinion that Amtrak is a major contributor to the pattern, since the decline is disproportionately heavy in the northeast corridor where Amtrak has

71

TABLE 24
CLASS I CARRIERS' OPERATING RATIO AND PROFIT, 1971–1976
(dollars in millions)

Year	Total Operating Revenue	Total Operating Expense	Operating Ratio[a]	Operating Profit Margin[b]
1971	$758.4	$664.4	87.6%	12.4%
1972	775.3	689.6	88.9	11.1
1973	814.6	738.0	90.6	9.4
1974	932.6	858.8	92.1	7.9
1975	941.5	880.4	93.5	6.5
1976	989.8	945.5	95.5	4.5

[a] Total operating expenses divided by total operating revenues times 100.
[b] Net percentage difference between operating revenues and operating expenses divided by operating revenues.
SOURCE: *The Intercity Bus Industry: A Preliminary Study*, Interstate Commerce Commission, Bureau of Economics, May 1978.

TABLE 25
CLASS I CARRIERS' REVENUE PASSENGERS, 1971–1976
(millions)

Year	Regular-Route Intercity Service	Local Service	Special Service[a]	Total Revenue Passengers Carried	Percent Increase (Decrease) from Prior Year
1971	129.0	18.6	19.2	166.8	
1972	127.3	16.2	20.4	164.0	(1.7)
1973	118.9	16.5	19.4	154.8	(5.6)
1974	126.3	17.0	25.4	168.7	9.0
1975	115.7	13.4	17.5	146.6	(13.1)
1976	107.0	13.7	18.2	139.0	(5.2)

NOTE: Totals may not add up because of rounding.
[a] Charter, sightseeing, and other.
SOURCE: *The Intercity Bus Industry: A Preliminary Study*, Interstate Commerce Commission, Bureau of Economics, May 1978.

TABLE 26

CLASS I CARRIERS' REVENUE PASSENGERS BY KIND OF ROUTE, 1971 AND 1976
(millions)

Service	1971	1976	Difference	Percent of Total Difference
Regular route intercity	129.0	107.0	(22.0)	78.8
Local	18.6	13.7	(4.9)	17.6
Special	19.2	18.2	(1.0)	3.6
Total revenue passengers carried	166.8	139.0	(27.9)	100.0

NOTE: Totals may not add because of rounding.

SOURCE: *The Intercity Bus Industry: A Preliminary Study*, Interstate Commerce Commission, Bureau of Economics, May 1978.

had its principal growth. Table 28 demonstrates that passenger-miles, passengers, bus-miles, and average loads all declined in the northeast corridor at rates well over double the rates in the rest of the country.

The damping effect of Amtrak's fare structure is evident on both revenues and revenue per bus-mile. Greyhound estimates that, accepting the estimate of 23 percent of Amtrak passengers as being

TABLE 27

CLASS I CARRIERS' CHANGE IN PASSENGER-MILES IN REGULAR-ROUTE INTERCITY SERVICE, 1971–1976

Year	Passenger-Miles (millions)	Percent Increase (Decrease) from Prior Year	Percent Increase (Decrease) Since 1971
1971	14,104		
1972	13,576	(3.7)	(3.7)
1973	13,898	2.4	(1.5)
1974	14,667	5.5	4.0
1975	13,169	(10.2)	(6.6)
1976	12,277	(6.8)	(13.0)

SOURCE: *The Intercity Bus Industry: A Preliminary Study*, Interstate Commerce Commission, Bureau of Economics, May 1978.

TABLE 28

COMPARATIVE PERFORMANCE OF PRINCIPAL NORTHEAST
CORRIDOR BUS OPERATIONS WITH REMAINDER OF COUNTRY, 1971–1976
(percent)

Passenger Miles	
Northeast corridor	−25.8
Other parts of country	9.2
Total country	−11.0
Passengers	
Northeast corridor	−27.4
Other parts of country	−11.5
Total country	−13.1
Bus Miles	
Northeast corridor	−16.8
Other parts of country	− 6.5
Total country	− 7.5
Revenues	
Northeast corridor	− 1.9
Other parts of country	+22.5
Total country	+19.6
Average Load	
Northeast corridor	−10.7
Other parts of country	− 2.6
Total country	− 3.6
Average Revenue per Bus Mile	
Northeast corridor	+17.9
Other parts of country	+31.1
Total country	+29.3

SOURCE: American Bus Association, based on carrier records and reports submitted to the Interstate Commerce Commission.

people who would otherwise travel by bus, Amtrak's existence costs the bus industry about $50 million per year in lost revenue from ticket sales.[18] This amounts to somewhat over 4 percent of the industry's gross revenues, which were $1,231.9 million in 1976.[19]

A federal estimate produced early in 1979 is consistent with a higher figure. The Amtrak Improvement Act of 1978 required the

[18] Estimate of Nicholas E. Bade, director of marketing, Greyhound Lines, Washington, D.C., July 18, 1978.

[19] Report from the American Bus Association, 1977, p. 26.

GAO to study Amtrak's effect on the intercity bus industry. The GAO considered the principal surveys of Amtrak and bus passengers, the experience of bus companies in the face of newly instituted services (notably, Indian Trails' experience when paralleled by Amtrak's Chicago–Port Huron train), and the econometric literature on the various elasticities of demand for surface passenger transportation. The finding was that bus ridership in 1976 measured in revenue passenger-miles would have been 14.8 to 29.5 percent higher in the northeast corridor and 4.6 to 9.1 percent higher elsewhere if Amtrak service had not been available. For the nation as a whole, the GAO concluded that major bus companies would have experienced 5.5 to 10.9 percent additional regular-route ridership in 1976 in the absence of Amtrak.[20] The depressing effect of Amtrak's existence on bus fare structures was not estimated.

Conclusion

In summary, Amtrak has been a failure because of the misconception on which it was based. Apart from the efforts of unions of railroad employees endeavoring to continue their employment and of railroad managements seeking to relieve themselves of their passenger deficits, the principal political pressure for establishment of Amtrak came from people who received a consumption value from travel on passenger trains. To see the luxury aspects of railroading decline more rapidly than patronage was intolerable to them, and they projected their views into a conviction that the decline in ridership could be reversed by improving the quality of the service.

Enjoying rail travel is a legitimate leisure taste, but the number of people who share this taste is too small for a policy based on it to succeed. The number of railroad enthusiasts, based on membership in rail historical and technical organizations, is probably between 100,000 and 200,000, too small to support even museum train operations without the demand of general tourists. Further, not all who are identifiable rail enthusiasts are given to intercity rail travel, and many oppose Amtrak's existence on economic grounds.[21] The affluent elderly are probably the largest group to which the policy of restoring ridership by increasing the quality of service could appeal, but this group

---

[20] "Amtrak's Economic Impact on the Intercity Bus Industry," General Accounting Office, Report no. PAD–79–32 (1979), pp. 26–27.

[21] On rail enthusiasm and Amtrak's political support's not being coterminous, see David P. Morgan's editorial, "The Amtrak Cult," *Trains*, December 1974, pp. 3–6.

atrophies, for it is mainly limited to the present generation of elderly. The next generation of aged will have been habituated to air travel for their adult lifetimes. Amtrak's largest single market in the long run is probably the people afflicted with fear of flying, a fear which Amtrak believes some 25 million Americans share.[22]

Evaluations of two of the state-subsidized services of Amtrak demonstrate the large consumption element in the ridership. The Minnesota Department of Transportation in January 1977 studied the first thirty-months' experience of the state-subsidized Minneapolis–St. Paul–Duluth service. The train was typical of the services operated under section 403(b), with an average ridership rising from 61 to 162 passengers per trip. Fares covered 36 percent of cost. The train had a heavy summer seasonal peak. The schedule originally provided for morning departures from Duluth with evening returns to allow shopping or business in the Twin Cities. This proved poorly suited to the demand, which was mainly of Twin Cities residents for recreational trips to the north. A schedule of morning departures from the Twin Cities was instituted, with a Friday evening ski train in season. The transit authority in Duluth scheduled a sightseeing bus in connection with the train.

In a survey of seven days' duration in September 1977, 44 percent of the riders reported that novelty was their reason for using the train. Approximately 90 percent responded that their purpose was recreation or vacation, and 75 percent responded that they could have gone by automobile. Of those surveyed, 98.9 percent responded that they had not made a trip to Duluth in the past year; only 1.3 percent of respondents were repeat riders. The Minnesota Department of Transportation concluded that the state expenditure of $7.23 per passenger was mainly a subsidy to the City of Duluth and to ski operators in the vicinity, and that the subsidy was a relatively inept one. It could be more effectively administered in fashions more direct than running a passenger train.[23]

A survey of ridership of Los Angeles–San Diego trains by the California Department of Transportation brought out similar information. The trains in this instance were three operated by Amtrak from its own funds, plus two operated with state funds under section 403(b).

---

[22] *Background on Amtrak* (Washington, D.C.: National Railroad Passenger Corporation, 1977), p. 5.

[23] Minnesota Department of Transportation, *Report to the Legislature on Amtrak Rail Service between Twin Cities and Duluth*, January 18, 1977, with cover letter of Jim Harrington, commissioner, to Senators Roger Moe and Clarence Purfeerst and Representatives Stanley Fudro and Fred Norton, January 26, 1978.

A sixth train was operated between February and August 1978 with Los Angeles County funds, but then taken over by the state. Consequently, the service is a relatively frequent one, with several intermediate stops.

Surveys of the ridership in 1976 and 1977 document the recreational nature of the service. More than a third of the riders were children on school field trips who were not counted in the tabulation. Business commuters were less than 4 percent of the ridership. The typical respondent made about ten intercity trips per year, with half by train—a frequency of train use of less than once in two months. Families using the train for recreation amounted to nearly half the riders, and 17 percent of the fare-paying passengers were under twelve years old. About 65 percent of respondents were on recreational trips, compared with 8 to 25 percent on business. Students and retired persons made up 35 percent of the respondents. The most frequent reason given for using the service was "Wanted to ride the train this time."[24]

More generally, the relative experience of the transcontinental trains versus the midwestern and western corridor service is consistent with the hypothesis that the Amtrak program is a subsidy of a form of consumption. As mentioned in chapter 2, when the initial Amtrak system was being planned, a large number of observers held that Amtrak's comparative advantage was for intercity services at short-to-intermediate distances, whereas the transcontinental services had already demonstrated themselves to be hopeless.[25] In a system that proved unprofitable everywhere, the transcontinental services did better and the corridor services in the Midwest and West much worse than anticipated. The train along the West Coast which was not even in the original proposed plan proved to be one of Amtrak's relative successes. The transcontinental trains and the north-south train along the West Coast which connects them provide a consumption value, while the corridor services provide relatively little. As Secretary of Transportation William T. Coleman pointed out, the long-distance services are in the nature of cruise ships, where travel is its own end.[26]

---

[24] California Department of Transportation, Southern California Association of Governments, and Comprehensive Planning Organization of the San Diego Region, *San Diego–Los Angeles Corridor Study Phase IIB* (1976), supplemented by Division of Transportation, *Ridership Surveys on Amtrak San Diegan Trains*, summarized by Renee J. Peyton, *Commuter Railroads in Southern California: An Economic Analysis*, Automobile Club of Southern California (1978).

[25] For expectations on the relative prospects of the corridor and long-distance trains, see "Alice in the Guide," *Trains*, March 1971, pp. 3–6.

[26] *National Transportation Trends and Choices to the Year 2000* (Washington, D.C.: Department of Transportation, 1977), p. 192.

The preoccupation with the quality of the service which was so apparent in the establishment of Amtrak was suitable mainly to the long-distance trains. This preoccupation resulted in the anomalous vesting in the Interstate Commerce Commission of control over the quality of service but not the rates, and it was at least partly responsible for the total neglect of attempting cost-saving changes in labor rules. The effect was to create a monopoly over the passenger train assuring that its operation would be labor-intensive and traditional. Had Amtrak not been established, some independent operators might have contracted with individual railroads, as Auto-Train did, to provide service in an innovative fashion on limited routes. This is by no means assured, since Auto-Train has been unprofitable since 1976, but we cannot know because Amtrak's statutory authority forecloses the opportunity. Notably, Auto-Train's own employees are nonunion, allowing a freer assignment between duties than the brotherhoods will permit.[27]

Similarly, the existence of Amtrak inhibits development of higher quality bus service. Because Amtrak is available to the people who demand a high quality of service in spite of a low valuation of time, bus service with reserved seats, on-board food and beverage facilities, or attendants is assured of the failure it has typically had.

The conclusion that Amtrak is a subsidy of a form of consumption of limited taste is also consistent with the political strength it has shown. The program is a rather extreme example of the oft-noted use of governmental processes to administer a benefit to a small group that is large enough to motivate them to fight for it, but at a cost so small per person to the electorate as a whole that there is negligible incentive for anybody to fight against it. This is consistent with Amtrak's support group's being so much larger than its ridership. President John P. Fishwick of the Norfolk & Western Railway observed, "People like to watch trains but they don't like to ride them, so Amtrak is not providing a system of transportation but a form of kinetic art."[28]

Given the ubiquity of this pattern of subsidy, it is superficially tempting to conclude that Amtrak will continue indefinitely. By reequipping the trains and building new stations throughout the country, the corporation has maximized the probability that Congress will accept a sunk-cost fallacy for continuing the system. The fact that Canada established a similar national passenger train system in

[27] *Trains*, December 1974, p. 23.
[28] *Trains*, March 1978, p. 11.

1976, when the failure of Amtrak was unambiguously apparent, is further evidence of the likelihood of the policy's continuation.

On the other hand, the political processes do not typically continue hopeless policies indefinitely. To pursue Secretary Coleman's analogy, the subsidies to American flag passenger ships have atrophied until only four vessels remain funded. The policy will probably end when these ships are retired. Amtrak will probably suffer a similar long atrophy and finally be discontinued. As mentioned in chapter 2, Secretary of Transportation Brock Adams at the end of 1978 and early in 1979 proposed reduction in Amtrak's route mileage by about 43 percent, but only a 13 percent reduction was made. Congress in 1979 enacted a criterion of net losses of no more than seven cents per passenger-mile for long-distance trains and nine cents for short-distance trains for compulsory retention in the basic network. Even though the purpose of this rule is to constrain Amtrak in its discontinuances, the effect in the long run will probably be to demonstrate the hopelessness of successively more of the system. The secular forces operating against Amtrak will render successively more trains unable to qualify for compulsory retention under the rule.

Whether or not further reductions are made in the immediate future, the system will probably atrophy in the remainder of the century to the northeast corridor services on Amtrak's owned track. These operations are usually thought to be closest to Amtrak's comparative advantage. Unfortunately, as the relative costs of rail passenger transport and its alternatives show, Amtrak has no comparative advantage. Such rivalry with air and road as it is able to present in the corridor results mostly from the nonprice rationing of roads and airport runways, which creates serious queuing problems on both, especially in the New York area. If variable user charges were in force, varying fees for the runways and roads by hour, the present peaking and queuing problems could be dealt with. Amtrak's apparent advantage stems from its using a private right-of-way that is free of these problems.[29] Similarly, Amtrak's principal revivals in passenger volume have resulted from the nonprice rationing of gasoline which creates occasional fuel shortages. This system is less likely to survive than the nonpricing rationing of roads and runways.

Amtrak's operations in the northeast corridor inflict maximum damage on rival carriers, particularly on the major bus routes. Its existence is the analogue of the newer urban rail transit systems. The Bay Area Rapid Transit, for instance, diverts passengers from the

[29] See Ross D. Eckert, *Airports and Congestion* (Washington, D.C.: American Enterprise Institute, 1972).

most heavily traveled routes of the Alameda–Contra Costa County Transit District, interfering with the cross-subsidy of crosstown lines by arterial routes. The consequence is to render the whole transit system inoperable except by direct subsidy.[30] Not surprisingly, the intercity bus industry has already begun to seek operating subsidy from the federal government.[31]

The National Association of Railroad Passengers explicitly favors greater coordination of the two modes, moving the longer distance passengers by rail.[32] One federal study of this policy has already been published.[33] The costliness of such a policy, however, is likely to engender further erosion of Amtrak's political support, making Amtrak's indefinite perpetuation even more unlikely.

---

[30] George W. Hilton, *Federal Transit Subsidies* (Washington, D.C.: American Enterprise Institute, 1974), pp. 102–103.

[31] U.S. Congress, Senate, *Financial Condition of the Intercity Motor Bus Industry,* Hearings before the Subcommittee on Surface Transportation of the Committee on Commerce, Science and Transportation, 95th Congress, 1st session (1977) esp. pp. 42–53.

[32] Letter of Thomas G. Crikelair, assistant director, National Association of Railroad Passengers, ibid., pp. 95–96.

[33] *Report on the Potential for Integrating Rail Service Provided by the National Railroad Passenger Corporation with Other Modes,* Department of Transportation, Report FRA–RFA–1–76–05 (1976).